D1551164

THE
RESTLESS
YEARS
1955-63

Cecil Beaton's Diaries
Volume Five

SAPERE
BOOKS

THE
RESTLESS
YEARS
1955-63

Published by Sapere Books.

11 Bank Chambers, Hornsey, London, N8 7NN,
United Kingdom

saperebooks.com

ISBN: 978-1-912546-41-1

Foreword to the New Edition

I welcome the republication of the six volumes of Cecil Beaton's diaries, which so delighted readers between 1961 and 1978. I don't know if Cecil himself re-read every word of his manuscript diaries when selecting entries, but I suspect he probably did over a period of time. Some of the handwritten diaries were marked with the bits he wanted transcribed and when it came to the extracts about Greta Garbo, some of the pages were sellotaped closed. Even today, in the library of St John's College, Cambridge, some of the original diaries are closed from public examination, though to be honest, most of the contents are now out in the open.

The only other person who has read all the manuscript diaries is me. It took me a long time to get through them, partly because his handwriting was so hard to read. I found that if I read one book a day, I had not done enough. If I did two in a day, then I ended up with a splitting headache! This in no way deflected from the enormous enjoyment in reading them.

Altogether there are 145 original manuscript diaries dating from Cecil going up to Cambridge in 1922 until he suffered a serious stroke in 1974. A few fragments of an earlier Harrow diary survive, and there is a final volume between 1978 and 1980, written in his left hand. 56 of these cover his time at Cambridge, some of which appear in *The Wandering Years* (1961). 22 books cover the war years, and were used for *The Years Between* (1965), and nine books record his *My Fair Lady* experiences, some of which appear in *The Restless Years* (1976) and were the basis for *Cecil Beaton's Fair Lady* (1964). These six volumes probably represent about ten per cent of what Cecil Beaton actually wrote.

The diaries attracted a great deal of attention when first published. James Pope-Hennessy wrote of Cecil's 'thirst for self-revelation', adding that the unpublished volumes were surely 'the chronicle of our age'. Referring to Cecil's diaries, and those of Eddy Sackville-West, he also commented: 'We could not be hoisted to posterity on two spikier spikes.'

I have to tell the reader that these volumes were not always quite the same as the originals. Some extracts were rewritten with hindsight, some entries kaleidoscoped and so forth. Certain extracts in these six volumes were slightly retouched in places, in order that Cecil could present his world to the reader exactly as he wished it presented. And none the worse for that.

Hugo Vickers

January 2018

Part I: Changing Perspectives, 1955

HAIRCUT

January

Hurrying up the marble steps with nimble alacrity towards the Men's Hairdressing Department of Selfridge's, my mind went back to the time — oh, crikes! how long ago was it? — when I started coming here to have my hair cut by nice, carroty Mr Massey. The expeditions as a schoolboy from Temple Court in Hampstead to the West End were always exciting and full of adventure. I really felt I was seeing life from the top of the bus as the bell ting-tinged down Finchley Road towards Baker Street and Oxford Street. Once the matinée idol, the fair, wavy-haired Owen Nares, jumped on board. As the conductor came towards him I had the full benefit of the Greek-god profile as I heard him, in his plummy drawl, ask: 'One to Piccadilly Circus, please!' It was a Wednesday and no doubt he was going to the theatre! What glamour life possessed!

London, to me, consisted almost exclusively of Selfridge's. Gosh, what a feeling of sophistication it gave me to sit on a high stool and drink a real American ice-cream soda! Then I bought a large packet of equally American peanut brittle, and prowled around the Photographic Department and other counters in the hope of seeing Gladys Cooper shopping. It was always here that Reggie and I had our hair cut. Thirty years must have elapsed since that time when first my younger brother affirmed, with utmost urbane authority, that no one in London cut hair so well as Massey. Sometimes I have migrated to Trumpers where there is always an uncanny and exclusive smell of orange hairtonic. But one is never given a welcome; one is rather grudgingly accepted as a client; and so I return to my tactful old friend in the large white emporium on the first floor of Selfridge's.

The usual talk: 'Has Mr Jack Gordon been in lately?' 'When was it that Mr Selfridge himself ceased to come here for his daily trim?'

As Massey turned me on the revolving chair to face the light from a huge window I saw my reflection in the glass opposite: I flinched. How could it be that I looked so hideous and so old? Had I really got such baggage under my eyes? Where did I get that bloat? It was not until the end of the haircut that I was pole-axed with the greatest shock of all. Massey pivoted me around again so that my back was to the light, and he produced a hand-mirror in order that I could see if he had clipped the nape of my neck to my satisfaction. I almost keeled over the edge of the chair at the sight in the reflected glass! A semi-bald man of twice my age and size sat in my place. I had not known that the hair on the crown of my head was becoming sparse. But this was a ghastly tonsure! I felt sick, as one does when an elevator rushes too quickly through space. Men suffer just as much as women at getting old and losing their appearance; every bald man is a personal tragedy.

Massey must have gauged the stricken horror in my voice as I moaned: 'It can't be as bad as all that! Oh, Christ! What can I do to be saved?' Massey nodded compassionately; trying to console me, but making the situation more tragic, he said: 'I shouldn't have let you see, should I? It was a mistake to do that, wasn't it?'

I crawled away down those marble stairs. The commissionaire asked: 'Taxi?'

'No, hearse please.'

THE RIVIERA

January 1955

Echoes of former glories persist along the now comparatively shabby haunts of the Côte d'Azur. A garden falling into a wilderness still possesses shades of King Edward VII; a crumbling mansion is a memory of the Duke of Connaught. A tall, locked gate leads to the shuttered Villa Léopolda where Cléo de Mérode, the *poule de luxe* with the Leonardo hair-do, gave her purity of beauty to the ugly and unpopular King Léopold. At the time of the troubles in the Belgian Congo the crowds shouted 'Cleopolda!' at the King.

In Nice the Hotel Negresco with its wedding-cake façade, though slightly cracked, is still like icing sugar in the sun. But the vestibule is almost empty. The Promenade des Anglais is sparsely populated with a few old cronies. The reaper has taken his toll, and economics as well as fashions have brought this sad change. Perhaps Monte Carlo is the last place where one can still see a few decrepit French dandies tottering on their last legs in crowsfooted shoes, stovepipe trousers, and curled trilby hats. Their hair is ginger-dyed and artificially waved; fingers are gnarled and heavily ringed. Women-folk are mere bags of bones with kohl-rimmed, blank eyes, marmalade wigs, tired tulle and wired linen flowers. They are the last survivors of the caricatures of Sem and Capiello.

Hidden away in various parts of the rocky coast are a few bastions of the old days of Edwardian glory. Muriel Wilson is pottering among her borders of antirrhinums and larkspurs. Today her 'Maryland' garden is a mockery of its past grandeur, and the house is seedy and sad. So much has passed since she first came out here as a dazzling beauty, bringing with her her staff of servants from Tranby Croft, of card-cheating fame.[1] She managed to escape the German invasion of France on a coal boat which took three weeks to reach Gibraltar; but her seventy-five-year-old butler remained behind to look after the house. The Germans did him no harm; he was too old to suffer, they considered. But after they had been in occupation a year a German soldier was shot in the village, so thirty-six Frenchmen, including the aged butler, were rounded up and taken to Buchenwald. The wretched man at the time of his arrest was wearing nothing but shorts and a summer vest. He was lucky to die of pneumonia after two weeks; others suffered for years before they died.

Also back on this golden coast is the wealthy widow, the whitehaired Lady Bateman, who was so upset when her Croesus-husband died that she went round the world six times. Princess Ottoboni, and one or two other hostesses of different nationalities, spend their time bickering and pouring down slime and abuse on their friends' heads. Watching the newspaper lists of deaths is an exciting game for these faded survivors; a point is scored each time they see they have outlived an old acquaintance. 'They say poor Violette is in a bad way — on the way out.' 'Guido Sommi has just died.' The tom-toms relay the news of the latest victim.

Even before the last war, the seasons switched and the popularity of the Riviera was confined to the months of summer. The dangerous, curving Corniche road was jammed with sports cars on the way from one *plage* to another; sunbathing ladies covered in Ambre Solaire, rich young girls

---

[1] Tranby Croft, the Yorkshire home of the Wilson shipping family where, during a weekend party graced by the Prince of Wales (later Edward VII), Sir William Gordon-Cumming was accused of cheating. The result was a scandalous case in which the Prince had to give evidence.

and boys, all dressed as sailors, brought millions of francs and pounds and dollars to the new owners of casinos and night-clubs. The old winter chateaux were ill-suited to conversion to summer usage, but small gardeners' lodges, or servants' quarters, were decorated by Lady Mendl, and once more the Riviera was rich.

But today there are few foreigners who can pay the outrageous prices; most people are in favour of a cheaper holiday in Spain or Italy. French visitors are of the working class who, since they now have a paid holiday, arrive on their bicycles from the North and camp out in primitive conditions on the rocks or swarm into the small hotels where prices and standards are low. The promenade is littered with rubbish, the rocks with the remains of primitive sanitation, so it is not surprising that even without demonstrations by the Communists against the arrival of the American fleet most of the American sailors would prefer to go home.

ZAZU: OBITUARY TO PUG DOG

April 8th

I am about to return from a three months' work-out in New York. During that time, Zazu, the amusing little pug dog who had made life so agreeable with her charming ways, had suddenly and inexplicably died. My mother wrote that she was so upset that for some time she could not bear to be in the house and went to London.

Zazu was bought from a woman who lived on our way out of town to the country. As we were shown into the house a champagne-coloured pug of diminutive proportions gambolled into the room with a lovely lilting gait. She was the personification of gaiety and impudence. Her kennel name was

Zazu. No doubt but that she must be ours. A cheque was signed; short talks about her foods and habits, and the woman kissed the little dog on the forehead as my mother gathered her up and into her life.

From the moment of her arrival there was seldom a dull moment in the Broadchalke house; Zazu provided an infinite variety of delights. One could not look at the expression on her face of wistfulness, cruelty and curiosity without roaring with laughter. The eyes were far apart; the decoration of nose and mouth was devilish. She looked like a velvety pansy.

Zazu became an immediate favourite. The squabbling servants made up their differences on account of her, and my mother became exhausted by her incessant playfulness; she had never known a dog with such determination and character. Zazu was excessively stubborn and disobedient, but in spite of her bad manners we adored her.

Her powers of invention were extraordinary. With her imaginative tricks, she gave a new dimension to life. All sorts of inanimate objects suddenly became dangerous weapons. A scuffle in my bedroom, and I would discover that Zazu had started to eat a large tube of white oil-colour paint. She tore at tassels, chewed pencils and boots, and her inquisitiveness when I went to the lavatory and flushed the toilet, or got into my bath, was positively frenzied. On a walk in the garden she was always excavating new undergrowth, or discovering some strangeness in the flower borders.

I would bore my companions with anecdotes about her. I relived the time she was locked by mistake in the lavatory and chewed the wallpaper; the afternoon of the garden fête when she ran like a demented devil among the village children; the way she would become quite frantic in her determination to rush up and down stairs to retrieve a thrown ball.

I know I will be pleased to get back home, but when I arrive in the hall at Reddish something very vital will be missing.

PARIS: LADY MENDL

Summer 1955

No one knows the real age of Elsie Mendl; some say it was over a hundred years ago that she was born in America. Until recently, she gyrated like a galvanised monkey and in order to maintain her physical flexibility exercised herself each day in a most frenetic fashion. These acrobatics were watched by her awed friends and admiring staff who applauded the climax, a *pièce montée* when Elsie stood on her head. However, one day disaster overtook her. At least one vertebra was wrenched out of place, and the poor old girl was never to be the same.

Looking extremely delicate, Elsie is lying on a velvet leopard-skin-covered sofa in the bathroom of her Paris apartment. It is a room filled with orchids in crystal vases, glass objects, mirrors and mirror-screens behind one of which is her *chaise percée*. Elsie seems to be getting smaller every month and is certainly prettier — prettier than she has ever been before. Not until she was eighty did she learn to smile; it is now a sweet smile.

Soon a bachelor from the United States is shown into the room, and kisses are exchanged. The confirmed bachelor explodes: 'Well now, my dear, I've got some news for you!' The usual flapping and confidential gestures and grimaces. 'I'm going to bring Mr Getty into your life, and he's so rich you just can't believe it!' Elsie's health is at once restored. Bolt upright, she asks: 'But can't we get him to buy my Coromandel screen?'

I photographed Elsie this morning. She has just recovered from her last face-lifting operation (only a month ago). The bruises are no longer Stephen's ink blue and dark red, and the stitches hardly show, but no-one is yet allowed to kiss her on the cheeks. It was a major operation, and only an incredible old bird like Elsie could undergo such a shock voluntarily, and through sheer discipline be able to withstand it.

At any rate Elsie has fared better than Cécile Sorel, the octogenarian Académie Française actress, whom I recently saw standing outside Maxim's in a revolutionary costume of black velvet and ostrich feathers. Her canary hair now bears no more relation to her head than a badly fitting, too small wig. She has a twitch. With an apparent effort she pushes the lips, enlarged with paint and at variance with their true contours, over the teeth in an uncomfortable moue. But the worst aspect is that the face has been pulled up so taut that the eyes pop and can never close; at night she must wear a black mask in order to sleep.

For her photographs Elsie wore an elaborate new ball-gown with a white tulle crinoline skirt. The hairdresser, Antonio, had done his best with the few remaining strands of hair — had dyed them mauve, fluffed them into corkscrews, and filled in with spangled bows. The chauffeur, upstairs for orders, was invited in to admire the result of so much time, energy and expense. Elsie paraded in front of him like a mannequin on a wire. She asked: 'Don't you think it's pretty, Leon?' Leon, the driver, truthfully said: '*Och, mais c'est un miracle!*'

Elsie telephoned from Versailles to invite me down to dine. Her accent was as strongly Bostonian as ever (which sounds, in her case, like Brooklynese — a 'doity-doid' for 'thirty-third'), but her voice was sad, frail and crackling. 'My dear, I didn't *know* there was so much human pain to be endured in this world. It's the spine, you see, and they can't take out the spine of a very old wummun. They can't do nothun but drug you, and I've never been much of a druggist.' When I arrived the butler told me she was sleeping.

I decided to go for a walk in the park of Versailles. The Hubert Robert avenues of vast dark trees were a triumph of symmetry; at certain points one came to the junction of eight avenues stretching to the statue-adorned horizons. Surely the French in the eighteenth century had reached their peak in ordering nature to current fashion? Returning to Elsie's entirely green garden, I wondered if she had not beaten even the eighteenth century at its own game? The lawns were like billiard cloth, the overhanging trees were 'set' in place by a great scene designer so that not a branch dare move. But the *clous* of Elsie's topiary garden were the trees cut into the shape of oversize elephants. These green animals were Elsie's last defiance at the contempt with which the Germans had maltreated her garden during the Occupation.

I remember coming down to see the house directly after the enemy had left, in order to report to Elsie, in her Californian refuge, on the damage that had been inflicted to her pinchbeck palace. Against the boiseried walls, where Elsie's carefully chosen Jacob and Cressant pieces had once been placed, it was a travesty to see modern brothel-furniture, and a naked electric light bulb hung where rock-crystal chandeliers had been. The cellar was ransacked, but I remember finding in a cupboard a mountain of Elsie's scrapbooks. These were filled with photographs of Elsie's décors, her parties, and social activities. They must have struck the occupying Huns as being particularly eccentric with Elsie always wearing the most

15

exaggerated costumes, posing in a variety of extraordinary guises, and nonsensically even giving the Fascist salute when on a trip to Rome in the early days of Mussolini.

Elsie, fired with ambition for the stage, had realised that she had meagre talent as an actress and had invented the profession of interior decorator. Her fame spread throughout the Ladies' Clubs of America; Paul Cravath invested her earnings in General Electric and she became as affluent as if she owned a gold-mine. Yes, in her own way, Elsie had been quite a phenomenon. Later scrapbooks showed her in the twenties. She travelled. When first she saw the Parthenon, she exclaimed: 'It's *my* colour-beige!' It came as a surprise to see a very juvenile version of myself with Elsie at a supper party near Cannes.

Elsie had been good to me: she gave me, a shy and completely unknown stranger, my first exhibition in New York. I had arrived in Manhattan at the height of the winter season in the boom of 1931, with a crateful of very English watercolours and caricatures of the London scene, and a portfolio of photographs. I expected that any of the great New York galleries would promptly give me an exhibition. It shows how wrong and *naif* I was. Elsie, who was still in business as the most highly paid of all interior decorators, came to my rescue. She suggested that I should exhibit my wares together with her furniture in her showrooms on Fifth Avenue. Thus began a friendship from which I have benefited much.

Elsie, in spite of her great age, always managed to collect newcomers to her circle who kept her young in spirit. For several summers she took a house in the South of France to which Oliver Messel and I, and a number of our friends, were constant guests. We found much to laugh at in Elsie's company. Situations were always surprising — often fantastic.

Oliver's imitation of Elsie's Boston accent, which is much like Brooklyn-Jewish, complete with masterful gesture and frown as she related some latest drama, was one of the funniest in his brilliant repertory. Although, like a vain child, Elsie bridled when she was applauded, she did not mind making people laugh at her. With her constant companion, a middle-aged American named Johnnie McMullin, she performed a sort of perpetual turn: it was an act of complete frivolity and artificiality. Their dialogue on returning from a visit to various maharajahs in India made us roll about with helpless laughter.

From Elsie's house in the Midi her guests would invariably go over to Maxine Elliot's huge Villa de l'Horizon for lunch and a swim. The statuesque Edwardian actress now lived in respectable and luxurious retirement, entertaining a great number of people who, somehow, all had handles to their names. Maxine dearly loved a duke, but she adored even more her large black and white monkey named Kiki. Others did not — for Kiki did not welcome guests, however aristocratic, and had been known to bite them. One morning Elsie and her party arrived, with the usual fanfare, for a swim and Maxine's special pink cocktail and Chinese biscuits. Elsie was laughing her grey laugh and everyone admired the achievement of her appearance: blue curls in a Syrian fringe under a shepherdess hat, muslin-tucked and ruched blouse, pleated skirt, her choker of pearls, her diamonds, her well-shod feet. Delighted with her success, she flailed her arms and legs about.

Suddenly the air was rent by a terrible ear-splitting scream. A violent death? A murder? No — Kiki had hold of Elsie's ankle. The scream was followed by a great plop and a splash. Elsie was nowhere to be seen. For a moment everyone was too horrified to move. Then, seeing Elsie's shepherdess hat floating on the surface, it was realised that Elsie could not swim and had sunk like a stone to the bottom of the pool. Then followed more splashes, and a little later several divers brought to the surface an utterly transformed creature: hair in rats' tails streaming over a purple face — her fakir-thin body now revealed in clinging rags. Maxine, a victim of high blood pressure and a weak heart, was also now purple in the face. We feared that she might forthwith have a stroke. Maxine was a woman with little humour, but in spite of her abject apologies she could not keep a smile out of her large, topaz eyes as Elsie, propped up by two stalwart men, stood while Johnnie McMullin held his handkerchief to her nose shouting: 'Blow, Elsie! Blow!'

Elsie was never a snob but, having a lesbian background she saw the advantages of an arranged marriage with charming but impecunious Charles Mendl, an attaché at the British Embassy in Paris. Elsie enjoyed comparative respectability, and helped the stature of her husband by becoming an impeccable hostess on a grand scale.

In her last years Elsie has almost become a beauty. The hard, dog-biscuity face of the early photographs has mellowed; the eyes have become kinder and more compassionate, and the skin, now stretched over her delicate cheekbones, has created an effect of carved ivory.

I came in from the garden and my forest walk. The other dinner guest, the American Howard Sturgess, had by now appeared. We awaited the imminent arrival of Elsie. Various white-gloved servants came in to alter the placing of a chair or squirt the flower-scented air with more oriental perfumes. In the distance a parrot squawking, a great rattle over parquet floors, and Elsie, at very high speed, was wheeled in sitting like an idol in her chair.

Elsie is magnificent — and knows it. She squeaks with pleasure at our compliments about her coiffure, her sparkling jacket, her new necklace. We drink dry Martinis immediately served on small silver trays with the same biscuits that Maxine Elliott patented in the South of France. Elsie's food is always imaginative and unusual. She makes rules — never any soup: 'Don't start your dinner on a lake!' An exquisite meal is served at a small circular table decorated with, paradoxically among the silver gilt and crystal, some rustic bunches of nasturtiums.

Later Elsie confessed: 'I've outlived my time. I realise it: I'm too old now. I ought to have died before the war; I've just been hanging on since then, and for someone who's led such an active life as I have, it's terrible to retire and take things easy, and try to preserve a little vitality.'

Elsie showed us tonight, in many little ways, something of the experience she has gained in a long life of hard work. Yet, up to the last, she has brought amusement and activity with her.

When the evening had come to an end for her — it was to be the last time that I was ever to see her — she bid us remain and drink another glass of wine as the night was young — except for an old lady. She was then lifted up to bed by the chauffeur, Tony. The sincerity of the demonstration of love on the part of the servants was a tribute to her qualities. The servants were not merely in attendance on a rich old woman whom they knew would soon die and, maybe, leave them a fat present; they were grateful that such a remarkable character had treated them with the greatest fairness and consideration over a long period.

The other guest, that delightful, charming Howard Sturgess (he too, like Elsie, to die so soon), in his foghorn voice said: 'Elsie was wonderful tonight. I shall always remember her in that little jewelled jacket, with the butterflies in her hair, sitting against the green of the garden in the twilight.'

Tony, the gloomy chauffeur, driving me to the station to return to Paris, said: 'She may have been wonderful tonight. That's because you were there and gave her an incentive, and she hopped herself up, but in the morning she won't feel so good. She'll 'ave a 'orrible 'angover!'

GRETA (FROM AMERICA)

Greta wrote lovingly of England where there is fresh air. She sent her love to 'little Mr Burton',[2] and country neighbours Juliet Duff, Simon Fleet, and Clarissa Churchill. I was surprised to hear that she had received a charming letter from my mother, and Greta asked that I should give her a hug without her knowing it was from her. She also enjoined me to give her best to Daisy Fellowes if I should see her. If I should see Queen Mary I was to say nothing.

REDDISH HOUSE, BROADCHALKE

Summer

The one English summer to remember for its sun: ceaselessly fine day after day, the heat almost tropical. After luncheon I lay out on the terrace, broiling on a mattress. I sweated so much that after an hour reading David Cecil on Dorothy Osborne I came up to finish the essay in the cool calm of my bedroom. The exquisite, alert prose inspired me but after a while I started to doze.

I woke to find the household's latest addition — a white and grey kitten — in a pose of abandon on the brown and white

---

[2] Hal Burton, who had been staying with me.

percale of a sofa. A more charming picture could not be imagined. A breeze came through the open window and rustled some of the flimsy pages of my play on which I had been working earlier. The kitten stretched itself in the most luxurious manner. I shared its enjoyment of the moment. High summer: slight breeze blowing, a cock crowing in the distance and hens emitting the sounds of sleep.

I made a mental inventory of my room. Typewritten pages had now been blown onto the floor; Truman Capote's book of short stories was open on a stool with other books (Denton Welch's *Brave and Cruel*, Osbert Sitwell's *Laughter*, and Colette's *Gigi*); by the telephone, which at that moment began to ring, the snapshots of Greta in the triple red leather frame which she had given me. The only disappointment of the summer is that she is not here to enjoy it.

A perfect summer's day in my garden. This is the day I think about when I receive a sudden summons to America. Is it worth signing a contract that will necessitate my having to spend months staying in impersonal, expensive hotels when I could be writing my diary on the lawns as now?

This is the day that compensates for weeks of winter cold and rain. The sky is unfettered azure. The trees are still salad-green, and the lawns and fields like Ireland (as well they should be after the months of rain we have had); the birds twittering, piping, chirping, chirruping and hiding. The hoots of the owl, which generally augur more rain, cast no jarring note, for the barometer shows that it will remain fine — if not forever, at least for tomorrow. On the terrace butterflies hover over the heliotrope, nepeta, and tobacco flowers. Flapping back and forth their wings, they are relishing the pollen with greed and unction. They congregate particularly on the flat plates of the sedum or ice plant-red admirals, cabbage whites and chartreuse yellows. They take their fill and then fly off, possibly through the muslin curtains of my bathroom where they flutter frantically from window to window, beating against the panes until my huge hand clutches at their powdery, panicky wings and imprisons them. Then, too terrified to move in the dark palm of my closed fist, they suddenly find themselves unbelievably fantastically free to fly to the top of the walnut tree or, even further, to the row of elms beyond.

It is a poignant, nostalgic time of the year with the knowledge that it cannot last forever. As a flame flickers brightest before it finally goes out, summer is putting on its finest spurt. But it cannot be long before the frost will gradually scythe everything before it, and the garden will go into hibernation for all those long partridge-coloured months. Already the early morning produces a thick, silver-skeined carpet of cobwebs — for the dew is heavy; even at midday it has only been partially consumed by the sun.

I hate to admit that my little house at Broadchalke is used only for weekends, even at the least rushed times of the year. Yet I am seldom able to be here longer than from Friday lunchtime until Tuesday. My London visits are so filled with work and appointments that I pity myself when there is no time to go to picture exhibitions, films or plays. But any tempting offer to remain for Friday evening in London is refused and nothing will induce me to return 'of a Monday', for I know how necessary it is for me to be in the country.

Here the pressure is relaxed; even if my windows are shut, the clear country air seeps into my soul. I am able to read, write and think, and it is here that I give my subconscious an opportunity to assert itself. Without these periods of gestation I would no doubt dry up completely. It is reprehensible and silly that seldom do I go out for walks by myself, or manage even to get beyond my precincts, but no one who lives in the City would ever realise how crowded is the day-to-day existence of country people. Apart from my own creative work, there is always something that must be done, or that would be nice to do. The man comes about repairing the thatch. (It's too expensive just now to do the entire roof.) The electrician wants to know where to put the plug points. Could we spare two hurdles from the wattle hedge? Sequestrene to be ordered, and a ham, and we're running short of tumblers for the bathrooms, and the sweet peas will want new bamboo this year.

ON DRESSING

Some of my American friends are appalled at the lack of care with which I present myself, collar awry and socks coming down. They say: 'A typical Englishman with two days' grime on his shirt-cuffs.' But I am rather pleased with this inevitable insouciance, and that for most of the time I get away with it. I know I look cleaner than I am; it helps to have a cold-beef-and-bread-sauce skin. Only when dog-tired do I have a second bath during the day. I consider a second bath a waste — unless, of course, I've been doing something strenuous, or have played tennis and got into a good sweat. In fact, I am so Scottish that I find myself saving not only bath water, clean clothes, and my beard, but also my energies. If alone in the country, and not likely to be seen by anyone, I take satisfaction in not scraping my chin for a couple of days. I often wear a dirty shirt and a twenty-year-old suit.

   When I relayed a little of the above to my country neighbour, Eddie Sackville-West, he was quite appalled. 'My dear, I dress just as carefully if I'm going to see no one. I dress for my own satisfaction, not for the somewhat doubtful pleasure of others!'

Some very young person said the other day how much he longed to have money so that he could go off and buy himself a lot of suits, silk shirts and cuff-links. This struck me as being surprising yet I suddenly remembered what a thrill it once had been to order a new suit of clothes. My first brown suit at Harrow was a milestone!

Young 'teddy boys', with their bright blue or scarlet corduroy pants, seem to show spirit, but generally men still go about in dirty old mackintoshes, shiny, striped City trousers, and greasy bowlers.

The English have not recovered from the war, and it shows itself in the torpor of their vestments.

MISS COMPTON COLLIER

July

Many of my adolescent glimpses of the grand world came through the photographs in *The Tatler* which bore the credit line 'Miss Compton Collier'. Other photographs that appeared in *The Tatler* were attributed to 'Rita Martin' and 'Lallie Charles', so why, I wondered, should it be '*Miss* Compton Collier'. Who was this lady? I was intrigued to discover her whereabouts but I knew of no one who had ever met her, and her name was not listed in the telephone book. Her photographs invariably showed us leisurely ladies caught in a silvery light, enjoying the herbaceous borders, clipped yews, stone garden seats and sundials of their country houses. Poring over these reproductions week after week I came to know Miss Compton Collier's taste extremely well.

When possible, she chose to photograph her subject standing on flagged paths, terraced steps, rustic bridges or by balustrades. Occasionally Miss Compton Collier would sprinkle a successful actress or two among her aristocratic sitters; but these, too, would be photographed as far as possible from the atmosphere of the theatre and would be found on holiday or holding a sheaf of corn, leaning against a rustic gate surrounded by cow parsley. My earliest family snapshots were mostly made in emulation of Miss Compton Collier.

It was many years after Miss Compton Collier's photographs had ceased to appear that I heard that she had continued her career with unimpaired zest, and each spring would send to people of high rank an itinerary of her summer tour stating that she would be in the neighbourhood during a certain week in case she were needed for an 'at home' sitting. I was intrigued to know that this mysterious lady still existed, so I wrote to ask if she would deign to include me professionally in her schedule and take some pictures of my mother and myself in the garden at Broadchalke.

Miss Compton Collier proved to be an extremely agile spinster of over seventy with a pale brown face of minor distinctiveness with the flesh solid and shiny. She was dressed in old-fashioned clothes, somewhat like a land girl of the 1914 war, with large felt hat and flowing skirts. She projected a personality that brooked no nonsense, and no interruption; her main objective was to seek out the nearest flagged path and the most lichen-mottled stone garden ornaments. A slightly forced giggle was part of her stock-in-trade. This softened any of her criticisms and enabled her to make all sorts of observations that, without it, might have caused offence; it was certainly not a giggle from the heart. I felt that Miss Compton Collier did not approve of the decoration of my house; she was only interested, and that for utilitarian reasons, in the bathroom, and the quicker outside the better.

Miss Compton Collier is extremely knowledgeable about gardens: 'After all, I have photographed eleven thousand of them!' She knows her England well: 'Dorset has the best little manor houses. Oxford is where the *nouveaux riches* live in gardens planned by Sutton's. That thatched wall is typical of Wiltshire; we must take it quickly — but, oh dear — the horrid sun is coming out! I hate the hard light it gives. Such a bad week last month — sun every day! I loved the summer before — rain all the time! People can't believe it when I photograph them in a downpour. But I say: "I'll give you your money back if you don't like it!"' Recently in Scotland she had placed a whole tribal family in the garden under umbrellas, and at a given moment ordered the gillies to rush up to take away the umbrellas while the exposure was made.

Miss Compton Collier took pictures of my mother and myself obediently sitting on an old stone seat with the dog at our feet. Behind the camera her performance was dynamic — even acrobatic. In order to stimulate the interest of her subjects she would jump up and down, wave an arm, squeak a rubber dog, and hum in a high musical voice. Suddenly, with a heavy click, the shutters of the lens would open and close. 'Got it!' shouted Miss Compton Collier in triumph. Her face was now a matter-of-fact, rather sullen mask. The switch from such inspired enthusiasm to the merely businesslike was somewhat of a shock.

At lunch she told us that for many a donkey's lifetime now she has lived in a small house in West End Lane, Hampstead, tended by an old servant of seventy-six. Miss Compton Collier appears so strong and healthy that one knows it is true that when she goes to bed it is to sleep so soundly that nothing will disturb her — not even a bomb. In fact, in one raid when the roof was blown off the house and all her rooms but two were destroyed, Miss Compton Collier went on snoring.

'Every day of my summer is taken up with work; from April to October I'm busy, so I leave everything else that has to be done to my winter months. I only do shopping in January: if a cup gets broken it has to wait till the first of the year. But I hate shopping in any case — it bores me. Now these clothes I'm wearing were bought fifteen years ago. I never read the papers: they're so vulgar. I've never listened to the radio; I hear everything I want to hear. And I wouldn't dream of doing the usual things like filling in a census or having a ration book — I just haven't time. I hardly ever go to a play, but when I do I ring up and find out first if it's got a nice happy ending because I hate all these squalid dramas that are so much the fashion. I loathe magazines and won't contribute to them any more now that they're full of Communist propaganda. I've never worked for the Press; if, in the old days, my pictures were used in *The Tatler*, it was I who chose the people to photograph: I never took people specially for the paper.'

'How did you become a photographer?' I asked.

'I had a weak heart at school and wasn't allowed to play games. Someone gave me a camera and I suppose that the artistic feelings, always in my family, came out in my generation in this different way. In another century I would have been a painter, I suppose. My great-grandfather sang at Queen Victoria's wedding.'

Miss Compton Collier does most of her own photographic processing, and said she was up till three o'clock last night developing plates. All her paraphernalia is entirely obsolescent. She climbs under a dark red velvet cloth attached to her yellow wooden 1895 camera with its long rubber tube with ball-shutter release. Hanging from the wooden tripod is a large bag containing a menagerie of toy dogs, mice and other pets to attract the attention of her aristocratic children and animal sitters.

Miss Compton Collier has never visited a photographic exhibition, and shows complete ignorance of the work of other photographers. She had never heard of the work of Steichen, Bill Brandt or Cartier Bresson. Although she has no further ambitions, she is never bored with her work; each sitting is a thrill for her.

In the silvery prints that resulted from her visit to Broadchalke both my mother and I appeared calm and leisurely, our faces smoothed and our hair silken. We were not only amused, but delighted.

MY MOTHER

August

Being the only unmarried member of my family, I have lived in close proximity with my mother all my lifetime. Although I have spent much time abroad, she was always the one to write to, to send my news, to come back to. In many ways my mother's tastes and mine are divergent. Sometimes I even feel we don't talk the same language. Naturally there is the usual disparity — that of two different generations — that comes between us, but perhaps an added trouble comes from the fact that I have found my way into a world that is not hers.

Sometimes I feel she is jealous and embittered; then I marvel that, at such an age, she has not developed more of the faults that often come with age. On the whole it is a relationship that is very close and harmonious and loving. It is also one of great duration, which only makes the inevitable end, which I will have to face one day, all the more unbearable.

She, more than I realise, is the one that I rely upon. She has wisdom, has had a lifetime of experience and she knows instinctively a great deal in matters of taste. She has always managed to run the houses we've lived in with success.

I am foolish enough to be influenced by a well-meaning friend who spoke highly of a fortune-teller. 'She is uncanny. Do go and see her.' I did. The birdlike little creature, dressed in the colour of raspberry fool, predicted the imminent death of my aged mother.

It was, therefore, with a feeling of great sadness that I came down to Reddish for my last weekend of the summer. Late August is a melancholy time of the year in any case, but some superstition had given me the feeling that perhaps this would be — after the fifty years of our life together — the last weekend that I would spend with my mother. In the light of my secret fear, her enthusiasms, convictions, energy, her economies, and her broad outlook on life appeared more poignant than ever.

Luckily it has been a quiet and pleasant weekend with summer sun continuing uninterrupted. The fields are yellow with barley and gold with corn, the hedges pale with spikes of long grasses, fronds of clover in full flower, and the trees are that dark, dark olive green that is almost black. My mother and I enjoyed the quiet. The stress of work was over, and now I had only to bother about tidying, packing the essentials, and, ineffectively rather, talking to the gardener about future plans. My mother, I was glad to hear, made many plans for next summer. 'We must have at least a dozen new roses — and I must order seeds — clarkia and more ranunculus. They've done well this year, and I didn't know we could grow them.' But her gardening knowledge is by no means confined to the ordering of plants. She knows exactly what has to be done to the earth, with the result that only a few of our things have failed this year. 'Gulliver should have thrown a bucket of water over those strawberry tubs in early May.'

Surreptitiously I tried to watch my mother, rather than, as is my custom, almost taking her presence for granted. I noted the intensity of surprise in her face as she appeared at the door of her bedroom to hear me ask at what height the carpenter should hang the baskets in the winter garden. I studied her look of amusement, or assumed terror, when confronted by the onrush of the army of Alys Essex's pugdogs. Most delightful was to see her from the top of the garden talking to Stacey, the jobbing gardener, as she walked along the lawns at such a brisk pace towards us. Accompanied by her own pug, she walked gracefully, sturdily, energetically as a colt. She is still wonderfully lithe and energetic, and she emanates an aura of well-being. White-haired, with remnants of great beauty, she is remarkable.

The 'winter garden' has mercifully been completed. I think much of the time spared to my mother will be spent in it at work on her tapestry. 'I'll never finish this needlework rug in my lifetime,' she says. 'Nonsense!' I reply half-heartedly. I tried to sketch my mother as she sat in the winter garden, surrounded by lilies in pots. But I was tired — worn out by the summer and by emotion. In any case, one sketch more or less — what is that in the face of life? I was sad, though, not to have some little picture that would be the perfect souvenir.

She was somewhat nervous in the car. She shied even at a signal marking a main road ahead; but we motored happily through the Chalke valley: Ebbesbourne Wake, Alvediston, Berwick, etc., down to the valley of Coombe — to visit the Freuds in their new greystone house. She remembered the Freud house in the days of its former owner, as she did the names of the gardener and the gardener's boy opposite at Swan Lake Cottage. As we drove along the Shaftesbury-Salisbury road, she remembered so much more than I did about the people who had lived around us at Ashcombe: 'That man Samson that kept the garage was a perfect brute. Mrs Mullin, such a nice woman, at the butcher's, always gave me lilies of the valley.' The summer day was almost painfully beautiful; the hills in a strange mist of heat. I got out of the car to pick a bunch of clover for my mother to give to Lucian. She said: 'You've got good eyes to see the clover so far away.'

VISIT TO THE MOROSINI

Venice: September 1955

When Venice was comparatively new to me, twenty or thirty summers ago, the Italian aristocracy continued to congregate, as they had done since the days of Canaletto, in St Mark's Piazza after the heat of the day was over. With eighteenth-century flourish they continued to greet one another with exaggerated nods and smiles.

I remember the buzz of excitement and the whispers: 'There's the Morosini!' as an elderly lady with dazzling white complexion, flaming hair under a large, hard hat, dressed in a pale salmon coat-and-skirt, grinned and bowed to left and right like a mechanical marionette. To a few fortunate ones she gave a brief audience; these remained at attention while she, grimacing, conferred upon them the accolade of her approval.

At this time it was difficult to believe that the Morosini had once possessed such beauty that she had become famous, but it was easy to surmise that she had been a great personality. I was intrigued to hear stories about her, many of them surely false, but all helping to create a legend.

The Morosini was said to have been more admired than any woman in Italy, and to have had many important lovers, amongst whom was the German Kaiser who, at the time she was living at the Cap d'Oro, had addressed one of his letters to her simply:

'To The Most Beautiful Woman

In The Most Beautiful House

In The Most Beautiful City

In The World.'

The letter is said to have reached its destination.

The Morosini's beauty centred on her brilliant turquoise-emerald eyes, her thinness of limb — an unusual attribute at this time — and her flowing red hair. By degrees, the brilliance of the eyes faded, the incandescence of the complexion was replaced by heavy applications of 'enamel', and the auburn tresses were dipped into a strong rejuvenating dye. A cruel rhyme was circulated about her:

Je suis la ruine en flammes

Et voilà mon épigramme;

Mais approchez sans crainte

Parce que, si la ruine est vraie,

La flamme est peinte.

The Morosini was of bourgeois origin, the daughter of a well-to-do Genoese banker. She had married a somewhat effete aristocrat whom, two years later, she dismissed. In an effort to maintain respectability at a time when women were not supposed to live alone, she brought her father to chaperone her. In spite of the beautiful daughter's desire for social success and for choosing her lovers less with her heart than her brain, and although surrounded by men of the greatest power, she remained suspect. Her love affairs became as notorious as her entertainments, but respectability still avoided her. It was only when her hair turned white, and she became lady-in-waiting to Queen Eleanor, that she achieved security. She had never been considered particularly witty but, with the passage of time, she became vivacious and full of fun. All through her life, and however lavish her parties, she showed an inability to be generous. Meanness dogged her throughout; in fact, it robbed her of her final epitaph: in order to economise on the fees she would pay for her portraits, she would employ second-rate painters. Instead of being immortalised in her epoch by Boldini, she decided on vast imitations by Salvatico (wearing a *tailleur* of the 1914 epoch, Parma violets and, inevitably, a large hat). Instead of Helleu, she sat to the Florentine, Corcus, who made a pale *art nouveau* nonsense of her in veils and mists and 1920 *bandeau*.

Brando Brandolini intimated one morning recently that nothing would be easier than for him to take me to meet the Morosini, and that it would amuse him to see my reactions to her. Since the former beauty now never emerges from her *palazzo*, having had the misfortune to break a femur, and must remain in an invalid's chair, she has become to the outside world even more of a legend.

At the end of a great hall on the *piano nobile* of a *palazzo* overlooking the Grand Canal, with shining, polished stone floors and high, echoing walls, there came an extraordinary series of parrot-like screams. As the volume of sound increased at our approach, a white-haired, painted woman with cherries and cream complexion, in black taffeta, was seen in the distance, waving and gesticulating wildly from her perch.

'Who are you?' she screamed in English. 'Who is this? Six of you — what a lot! ... Brando and Charlie Bestigui? ... And who are you? ... Oh, Ode de Mun and Freddie Cabrol and Daisy ... And who are you? ... Oh! — are you the English photographer who took the Coronation? Oh, you're very chic, very elegant!' Gales of convulsed laughter.

The aged beauty, eighty-nine years of age, wielded a stick and fluttered her large, black fan like a great actress who knows that the curtain is up and that the Goldoni comedy is under way. She relayed the tattle of Venice. Gossip is her passion and keeps her going: from early morning until two o'clock each day she is busy screaming into the telephone. She knows who is leaving, who is arriving, and not only who is sleeping, but who is dining with whom; it is a life of eighteenth-century intrigue and plot.

Footmen poured glasses of raspberry or redcurrant juice, or tipped cream into coffee. An incessant stream of visitors arrived. The old lady gave the impression of merry sweetness and loving kindness. But at no time had she been particularly endowed with either of these qualities; always she had shown a healthy respect for important people and an inflexible indifference to others. She could always laugh at herself and was the first to relate how, in a desperate attempt to improve the service in her house, as soon as she heard of the death of one of her best friends she telephoned to the butler, before the cadaver was even laid out, to know if he and his first footman would come into her household. It was after her fifth call that the butler ordered the telephone to be taken off the hook.

The Morosini continues to flash her fan above the splashing waters of the Canal. Perhaps only now has she reached her apotheosis. She has everything she needs; happiness exudes from her. She has acquired an audacity of speech and a frankness that comes with either extreme youth or partial senility.

TASTE CHANGES

Frosca Munster, who has come over from Paris, asked: 'Have you read *The Arabian Nights*?'

I was rather surprised at her question. 'I suppose I read it when I was growing up, but I've forgotten about it.'

'Well, you must re-read it now. You will thank me for sending you into the most delicious world. You will be so happy all the time you're reading. It's like a holiday. Incidentally, all of Picasso is based on these stories — the Cyclops, the magic caves. They're enchanting.'

Frosca and I then discussed the question of 'timing', and Peter Watson said that certain books he had lately re-read had given him such a completely new impression that they might have been entirely different from those he had read before. So much depended on one's attitude and susceptibilities of the moment. Certain books one loathed in the past became one's favourites later on; the disappointment at others is sad; and so with many aspects of taste.

It is interesting how, when one discovers a certain author, one invariably finds that one's friends have also picked upon the same writer at the same time. I do not know why I have never before read the Goncourt journals; but, since they have now made a great effect on me, I find that others suddenly share the same passion. Likewise, if by chance I come across Max Beerbohm's remark about never having met anyone who had boasted of dining last night with the Borgias, so next day in conversation someone will quote this same witticism.

The dark colours and sombre restraint of my mother's taste revolted me when I was a child. A certain cretonne in rather bold colours, which she chose to cover a French chair, appalled me; I now think of it as of an extraordinary and strange beauty. I consider it was a miracle that she should have found it. So it is even with plants and the flowers in one's garden. Thirty years ago when Lovat Fraser designed Polly Peachum's costume for *The Beggar's Opera*, I thought there was nothing more beautiful than candy pink roses. Now I am sick of them and prefer the pale flesh-coloured opalescent ones.

It is not just a surfeit that creates this desire for something different. It is less gratuitous than one imagines. There must be some dynamism, some inner urge, which creates a need and makes itself felt in many different directions all at the same time.

FRYERN: THE JOHNS

Autumn 1955

I have been working concentratedly for too long — result: I am like a fenced-in animal, seldom migrating beyond the confines of my terrace. Realising my staleness, I telephoned the Johns near Fordingbridge and proposed that I should come over forthwith and see them. At Fryern, the delightfully ramshackle, well-proportioned house in which the John family live, you always come across the unstereotyped or unexpected. In flat-toned, unenthusiastic growl Dorelia, or Dodo (Mrs John), answered my call and said it would be all right for me to appear any time — not a very warm welcome; but then this beautiful and remarkable woman is the very antithesis of a 'gusher'. She is particularly unforthcoming on the telephone.

I got into the car knowing I was about to enjoy myself. The sun was slanting over the hills before going in after a splendid day of late autumn. Mounting high over the downs one single magpie flew across my path.

I spat superstitiously and recited: 'Curse you — where is your mate?' But my spirits rose higher as I motored through the pretty villages of Martin, where Gainsborough lived for a time in a low timbered cottage, and Damerham, where the Japanese anemones were still flourishing outside the grey-stone and thatched houses. (One forgets that with the Michaelmas daisies, petunias, dahlias and chrysanthemums there is more colour in autumn cottage gardens than at any other time of the year.)

Past the common near Fordingbridge I took a wrong turning — I always do — but eventually the scene became familiar and I drove past the hideous 'modern' block that is Augustus' 'second' studio, and arrived at the late eighteenth-century house. I went through the open front door, past the Modigliani sculpture and the inconsequential clutter in the hall, and, looking into the large sitting room, found nobody. The walls were covered with paintings, a cat slept on a sofa. It was in the dining room that I found Dodo and Augustus sitting at the long refectory table littered with the remains of a large tea and lots of tobacco ash and cigarette stubs. It is a marvellous room: typically 'Dodo' in taste with its vast dresser, stretching the length of one wall, filled with every sort of china, pots of preserves, and assorted objects. On the walls a mass of various paintings by Gwen John and Augustus and Matthew Smith. A great white head of magnolia *grandiflora*, cut from the tree that pressed against the tall window-panes, was in a big pot waiting to be painted by Augustus.

Dodo, whose appearance is always an inspiration to artists, today seemed like a Tanagra figure in her Chinese-pagoda straw hat that she had bought in Fordingbridge. Augustus, puffing away at his down-turned pipe, wore a beret and a dirty blue smock and looked like a figure Manet would put into his views of the outskirts of Paris.

The atmosphere was quiet, relaxed. With the Johns were two strangers: a rather self-effacing 'art' enthusiast with his meek young wife. The conversation was about the gipsies in Spain. Augustus is by nature extremely shy, and it takes considerable effort on his part to make conversation. In fact he will not attempt to indulge in small talk, so there are apt to be long pauses between the topics. The visitors were obviously having a hard time; as people who are not experienced in the social ways of the world often do, they made too much fuss about their imminent departure.

In the John world there is never insincere *politesse* or phoney flattery; it is somewhat overwhelming to people who aren't accustomed to honesty on such a bold scale. Augustus is a monolith, a giant, and everything about him is grandiose: his Falstaffian bulk, his generosity, and his love of his friends. He is overflowing with affection and, like a great polar bear, likes to hug and kiss playfully almost anyone he finds sympathetic and congenial. He takes violent dislikes to people he considers pretentious or 'stuck-up'. He is a great iconoclast, and smashes sacred cows with superb gusto. He likes 'earthy' people and gives short shrift to the intellectuals. He can be caustic in his debunking, and sometimes his tongue is cruel. (Of his taciturn son, Edwin, he said he was the greatest linguist in silence.) But he can be kind, cosy and full of merriment. He is always quick with a witty answer. We were eulogising the nobility of the head of the Duke of Alba, who has recently died and of whom

Augustus had made several drawings. Augustus added: 'And his daughter is rather a wonderful creature to look at, too.' 'Oh no,' I disagreed, 'to me she was very disappointing!' To which Augustus, taking a great gulp of smoke from his pipe, murmured: 'It all depends what you wanted of her.'

Augustus hates 'rough' stories but cannot refrain from being quite frank even at the risk of shocking. A lady with a 'high society' drawl asked him how many children he had.

'Oh, about six or seven.'

'And what ages are they?'

'All about the same age,' came his bored reply.

Dodo has had a difficult life with Augustus' infidelities, his bouts of drunkenness and his open-handedness with money. Although Augustus has made a great deal there seems never enough left for the housekeeping. And the John household, with so many illegitimate children at home, has always been a large one.

He does not consider that it is anything but flattering that he should 'make a pass' at any sitter whom he admires. The 'pounce' is part of the sitting: the pose, the rest, the pounce, then on with the pose. Augustus is always hopeful that the pounce will succeed; but perhaps he knows from the start that it will not amount to much, for he never shows annoyance or is in any way hurt when rebuffed. Yet he would never give up trying, and, quite recently, a young sculptress to whom he was sitting for a bust was asked for how long she wished him to pose. At the appointed hour for the sitting to end, Augustus looked at his watch, unbuttoned his trousers, and presented to the girl a seventy-year-old, but still stalwart, phallus. The girl later confided that the sure way to prevent a half-hearted attempt at rape was to appeal to Augustus' very vital sense of the ridiculous.

But Dodo never worries. She loves Augustus and knows that even when it is vitally important for him to finish some portrait he will be lured away to the pony rallies in the New Forest or to ride over the downs and join a village pub crawl.

A neighbour told me of an argument that Augustus had with Philip Dunn, a very rich and brilliant money-maker, with whom he was dining at the Eiffel Tower in London. This was the expensive restaurant, presided over by the great character, Stulik, where Augustus when in London was most likely to be seen. Philip suddenly said: 'I'll bet you whatever money we have in our pockets that you are wrong.' Philip found that he had about twenty pounds in his own pocket. To his astonishment, Augustus laid down eleven hundred pounds in crisp, white, high-denomination notes. Stulik, the Hungarian proprietor of the Club-Restaurant, who had doubtless run a 'tick' with Augustus that had mounted with the years, had eyes like a rocket. In a flash the vast Stulik was hovering over the pile of money. Philip, when he had recovered from his surprise, said: 'You'd better let me have that money to invest for you.' But neither Philip nor Stulik got their hands on any of it, neither would Dodo be given a note of it. Augustus summed up: 'I like carrying a bit of pin money on me.'

The daylight faded. At last the strangers departed. Dodo produced a bottle of red wine and some thick glasses. We sat in the semi-dark and drank, and talked about the Renoir and Matthew Smith shows at the Tate and of the recent acquisitions to this very lively gallery. It was interesting to hear the venerable couple sadly shocked and baffled by the pictures which are now encouraged: one era again giving way to another. Augustus, very tactful and oblique in his criticisms, showed himself no admirer of Graham Sutherland: 'seems to pay little attention to the classical requirements of draughtsmanship.'

Dodo, less euphemistic, said of Lucian Freud: 'His women have these terrifying pop eyes and over-lifesize heads — they frighten me.' Augustus continued: 'But Francis Bacon doesn't know how to paint surely? What are those awful worms, and who on earth would buy that dog?' (To me, Bacon's 'Dog' is one of the most unforgettable pictures and unlike anything one has seen before.) Yet neither of these experts concede much quality to painters like Annigoni. Augustus surmised this 'show off' painter as having 'no balls'. Augustus can be extremely jealous.

It is curious that Augustus who, only a comparatively short time ago, was considered 'beyond the pale' — a revolutionary, a menace, a scandal — should already himself be on the other side, and inveighing against the 'new look' in painting and in manners. Augustus, for all his gipsy-vagabond aura, has perfect manners. He is quite formal on occasion, as when he carves the joint for a family gathering, insisting that the younger members serve their elders.

We were now sitting in complete darkness as we talked about friends and eccentric characters we all knew. Augustus laughed about his various vicissitudes with Louisa Casati, to whom he had periodically given a bottle of whisky and to her cat a rabbit. Augustus can be quick-tempered when rattled or riled; but to old friends he is always understanding and generous.

The moment came to turn on the lights, and for me to leave. I felt extremely exhilarated and happy after being in such congenial company. Dodo and Augustus always remain at their front door, waving, until their guests are out of sight. They made such a delightful Darby and Joan picture tonight, silhouetted against the brightly lit little hall — he, so monumental, she decorative in her hat and long skirts, waving by his side.

MOUTON ROTHSCHILD

Mouton: November

It is winter in England but it is like summer here — flowering Judas, chestnut, cherry and laburnum trees, wisteria rampaging, flowerbeds spilling bachelors' buttons and pansies.

My bedroom: *Louis Seize* bed painted white, *toile de joue* upholstery on white-painted furniture. Chinese pots containing lilac, plants in earthenware pots and saucers.

Through the shutters the sun pierces and makes incandescent the silver ink-pot, the strips of brass inlay on the writing table, and discloses the work of a small spider whose silver thread is weaving a pattern attached to the lilac.

The sound of hundreds of doves on the huge, sloping roof cooing with content, the clapping of their wings (applause in flight), deep guttural voices of those working in the stables and vineyards, a saw wheezing, a hammer on wood. Someone, in a burst of whistling, crunches over the gravel.

The vineyards have been kept for three thousand years. The stony earth sprouts fresh, strong shoots of vine. A Roman villa stood where Mouton now stands. With its cellars, its out-houses, stables and barns, it had been converted in 1922 from the seventeenth-century 'caves'.

The little villa-house where Pauline and Philippe[3] live today was built in 1890; with its tall Gothic stone walls, it is like a child's illustration to Walter Scott. Inside it is crammed with Napoleon in decorations, bead pictures, bead cushions, gold drawing-room furniture upholstered in scarlet brocade,

---

[3] Baron and Baroness Philippe de Rothschild.

flowered rugs on red carpets and coloured glass-panes in the veranda porch.

Huge trumpet-shaped vases, filled with blossom, stand on the floor and there are pots of calceolarias and ferns. Miniatures in jewelled frames are mounted on velvet and displayed on easels.

There are many dogs. Philippe says: 'A dog in the home is a piece of moving furniture.' 'What's the time? Oh, only an hour-and-a-half before dinner. That's not enough for pottering about my room and I must read the last act of a play,' says Philippe.

Bravo! Robert! The applause is for the flower decorations on the dining table. A raw-boned youth in white, starched jacket gives a twitch of pleasure and a subservient nod. Philippe says he always insists on having a different arrangement of flowers on the table for every meal. Another youth brings in a freshly ironed napkin, unfolds it with ceremony, lays it on the floor, then brings in the dog's dinner and places it on the napkin. M. le Baron, in claret velvet jacket and white satin tie, is robustly appreciative of the *petits soins*. Pauline asks: 'What are these called?', flicking a delicate hand towards the embroidered tablecloth which has been dotted for the occasion with sprigs of bridal wreath and laburnum surrounding a centrepiece of iris and chestnut blossom. It is a work of imagination. 'And he's just a simple peasant boy from here. He's never been further than Pauillac,' says Philippe, rubbing his outstretched hands as he settles down to his place at table.

A miraculous meal is served. 'To be greedy in this house is considered a form of politeness,' Philippe says, but unfortunately he must ignore the soufflé, so too the other dishes. His doctor forbids him to indulge. Elaborate dishes are taken from the table minus only one spoonful. Pauline toys with some watercress salad. It is the ritual that she enjoys and the opportunity for serious conversation. Tonight the subject is Izak Dinesen, Baroness Blixen, the one and only great literary star in Denmark 'who has all the Danish assets'. According to Pauline no woman writes about men as well as she. Her dialogue is always convincing. Dinesen seems to dislike women. Sometimes she invites seven men to dine. Yet, according to Pauline, although she tells an anecdote extremely beautifully in a man's deep voice, there is something less interesting about her personality than her writing. When she left Africa after having lost her lover, her husband and her money, she told a friend that she could do three things: she could cook, write, or become a tart. (Pauline considers forty to be an excellent age for a tart.) Dinesen decided that writing was the least hard work.

To some, Pauline seems affected, but her affectations have become completely natural. She has a rare capacity for concentration, and she expects others to listen to her with the same intensity that she would give to them. She is direct and purposeful. When one is not following her, she challenges one and proceeds to contradict if one's reasoning is hazy.

Pauline has come to rest in a well-lined nest. She has had a life of great contrasts — an unsuccessful marriage, a period of selling jerseys in Formentor, and various romantic attachments which led her to all parts of the earth and to no particular world. Yet Pauline has always known what she wants. Others may not have wanted Philippe, but Pauline was certain she knew he was for her. When she was introduced to him, she said with reverence: 'Not the poet!' and that flattered him above all else.

Pauline still has signs of independence. In Paris she lives in her bachelor apartment away from her husband's house in the Avenue d'Iena. She goes to Rome to learn how to draw; she has a model to pose for two months in the same position; thick portfolios are filled with drawings of the same subject. 'You can't have a teacher for this sort of thing: you must work things out your own way.'

Yet Pauline is deeply enmeshed with her husband's interests. Her eyes look meltingly at him; she laughs at his worst jokes, ignores or does not notice his interruptions. Philippe drops a fragment of food onto his dinner jacket, scrapes it off and eats it. She becomes tired; Philippe's vitality is excessive, but that is no complaint; Pauline, besotted, smiles.

Pauline is never hurried, never impatient; she loves to idle, to sit on a stone wall and watch the antics of her terriers. Meals are late: luncheon at two, tea at seven-fifteen, dinner nine-thirty. She is impervious to the passage of the months. A sofa, a room, an apartment, or a new building will take a long time to finish — a year maybe — but she has a five-year plan, a seven-year plan, a ten-year plan. She is not afraid of the future, or of loneliness; she takes her design for living for granted. If it is too exquisite, too refined for more earthly mortals, it has its own reality. She is an artist in life. She has the variety of an actress's inflections in her voice, sometimes so lightly skimming over the parenthesis then hitting the important word hard. Her gesticulations and arm movements are over life-size.

Twilight. In the sweet-smelling barn the oxen are at rest eating their evening meal. Silently they lie in the hay, so large and placid they appear as if they must be going to give birth. They chew the cud, and contentedly watch their golden world; this is their reward for their labour. A little man with shaggy grey hair prods the oxen in line. Obediently each rises, turns, and drinks deeply from the trough of fresh running water. They drink with such deep reverent seriousness; one can sense the cold, clear water going down the large trunk-like neck. Their drink over, they look sadly baffled. They turn around again, then manoeuvre themselves into their byre, sinking again amongst the hay to enjoy, at the end of their long day, peace. At four o'clock in the morning the shaggy-haired little man will prepare them for their work in the vineyards.

A deep emotion strikes within one. These beasts of burden are so beautiful in their pale dove-coloured hugeness: immaculately clean, soft, so strong. Their eyes benign and sad. These great beasts convey all the contentment but all the pointlessness and unhappiness of life. Suddenly I felt an onrush of tears. These wonderful animals will be slaughtered when their years of work are over.[4]

DIANA VREELAND

Diana Vreeland, cranelike, pink and white and black, is one of the people I most cherish. To be with her is like quaffing handfuls of mountain spring water: so invigorating and fresh. She is not only good, with a sense of values that is rare in the trashy, commercial world of fashion in which she works, but she has imagination and understanding of other people's troubles. She is one of the best friends that I possess. Some people do not understand her. Those who consider themselves living in a world of sophistication are worried by her unexpected originality. Conventional people confuse her outward image — the flamboyant appearance — with the truly civilised creature that she really is. But she does not stress her

---

[4] The oxen are now superseded by tractors.

serious side; in fact she spends much of her time in consciously entertaining her audience with a brilliant act of clowning.

When, soon after my arrival, I made my customary telephone call, she treated me to flights of glorious fancy. Diana the great eccentric: 'We've had the Comédie Française here. Such acting! It was immaculate! None of the tradition of grease paint and dirt, but the most pristine white gloves you've ever seen! If I could manage to have gloves like that, I'd be happy. But they were white, white, white, and when one of the men made a gesture with his hand, it was an unforgettable moment in theatre history. And the backs of their necks were so scrubbed!' Diana then gave me a detailed description of a new washing soap only to be found in Switzerland called 'Baby Blanc'. 'Believe me it is going to change our lives entirely!'

Then proceeding to what in others would be a more prosaic matter she informed me that Reed, her adored and adoring husband, and she had recently moved into their new apartment. 'But it's nothing like ready! We have six workmen here all the time, and they're so goodlooking, they're killers! And they're so young! They were all in the Navy together, and they have blue eyes and that wonderful look that people get when they haven't a roof over their heads. They're killers! But Billy Baldwin, my decorator, says: "Now, Diana, you've got to stop having a love affair with these men, otherwise we'll never get them out of the house and you know the job's got to be done."'

Diana Vreeland has become with the years one of the great personalities of the New York scene.

FISHING IN FLORIDA

The tug on the line, then the pulling in of this great, struggling weight. Exciting, yes. But the sport, for me, is overshadowed by the suffering of the fish. At the end of a merciless trip pulled through the relentless barrage of water, with a hook in its mouth or down its stomach, it is brought into a new, airless sphere, clutched at by terrifying hands while the hook is painfully, laboriously, extracted. Possibly a pair of pliers have to be brought into play to wrench the metal from the bone. Finally, the wounded fish is thrown to the bottom of the boat, where it leaps and darts in the terrible unaccustomed heat of the sun, while the fisherman is busy putting a new piece of bait onto his hook. It is when the line is thrown into the water that the fisherman turns, picks up his last victim, opens the lid of the cold storage chest, and throws the fish into darkness. Here it thrashes itself upon the corpses of its fellow denizens who have already suffered the inevitable. But the thrashing is of no avail; yet, suddenly, in a last desperate attempt to survive, it jumps and twists and turns somersaults in a panting frenzy of desperation. Then silence.

The serene fisherman waits patiently for another bite. As much as twenty minutes later, the fish in the dark chest makes its last terrible effort for survival. Bringing all its strength to bear, it is flailing itself in a useless agony until, at last, it subsides into its death silence.

Fish are said to have neither brain nor warm blood. Yet have we not witnessed that they have feelings, and must suffer in their death throes? Few fishermen give thought to hit their victims over the head in order to bring possible misery to an end. Meanwhile, such suffering continues everywhere, every day, every hour, every minute of every day.

MARGARET, DUCHESS OF ARGYLL

I'm tired of seeing Margaret about 'everywhere'. She always looks wonderful, but always the same, with her dark eyes and nut-brown hair, her pink and white complexion, her bandbox fresh dresses chosen with impeccable restraint. There is nothing of the private faces in public places about her. There is a dull inevitability and monotony about her beauty.

I was leaving New York once more by ship, and there was the usual dockers' strike. Going up in a luggage lift in the company of a bunch of fellow passengers, I was appalled to find myself standing next to Margaret. Oh, God! Would I have to be her companion for the next five days? I was a bit taken back when she asked if we could eat together during the voyage in order to escape the boredom of certain of her friends. What on earth could one find to talk about all the time? I believe it was the late Lord Wimborne who said of Margaret: 'She don't make many jokes, do she?'

Soon after the hooting and moaning of sirens, and as we were slowly passing 'down-town' Manhattan, I ran into Margaret sitting upright at a table, watching through a dirty window the skyline of Wall Street passing away from us. She had about her an extraordinary air of leisure and self-completeness.

'I always love to watch New York like this. Even if we arrive at six in the morning I come up to watch. I *love* New York. I feel so well there; it's a tonic for me. I'm always sad at leaving. But [surprised and startled] these windows are dreadfully dirty. Do they realise they haven't been washed for days? That's not too good, is it?'

I was amused at her apparent shock. Today most smart ladies are no longer surprised to see dirty windows. When I told Margaret I had intended to economise and have some of my meals in the dining room and not pay extra each time I go up to the Verandah Grill, she was equally shocked.

'Oh, but I love sitting with the sun shining and all the windows onto the sea. I can't bear eating during the day in electric light! Promise me to be in the Verandah Grill at one!'

Margaret was already sitting, cool and serene, when I went up. She was surveying the sea with a certain wide-eyed amusement. I discovered she has the capacity to be 'on' to herself.

I have known Margaret since she and my sisters were schoolgirls together, but I have never spent much time hearing her talk. I discovered that her idiom of speech is extremely fashionable. Her language is quite strong. Some particular man she described as the 'President of the Shit Club'. She explained: 'There's no nonsense about me. Oh no, I'm earthy: you can't fool me. I'm shrewd and have lots of common-sense which is very rare. Why do they call it "common" when so few people have it? No, I'm master at calling people's bluff, making them come off their perches; but I can't keep my great mouth shut. It's terribly hard for me not to contradict even when I know it's no good to do so, and I'm always putting my foot in my mouth. Queen Gaffeuse.' She admitted her clothes are the result of inordinate care and thought, that she buys them in New York because they're better value, but goes to Paris to keep her eye in. 'I love the way American women look — that neat, clean, simple look — but I couldn't be that. The overdressed type, that's me.'

Margaret must be one of the few left today who still feels impervious to the approach of the common man. Her money has given her a sense of security, and she is one of the rare examples of someone who has used it well.

'I'm a very good housekeeper. I run my home beautifully. I entertain a lot, but I don't think any woman should spend more than five minutes a day talking about the arrangements; it's too dull. But men hate the fact that I do it all so quickly. I talk to my cook on the house telephone each morning, but I wouldn't dream of going down to the kitchen. She knows that I can't boil an egg, so what would I tell her? I hate it in America where nowadays your hostess puts on an apron and says she is going to fry a steak. I want other people to do the cooking, and I can't bear it [*apropos* a visit to a Cabinet Minister] when people mow the lawn. They should get others to cut back the roses and dig.'

I discovered Margaret has quite a talent for observing her particular sort of existence, and drawing definite conclusions. 'American women are too sure of their husbands: Englishmen too sure of their wives.' 'French women spend their days sitting on the *bidet*.' Poor-little-rich girlisms: 'I love to dance, better than to eat.' 'I love camellias, but I don't like to see them growing.' 'Oh, do look at Lady Rosse with amber necklace and diamond bracelets and sapphire brooch. Oh dear, she hasn't thought that *parure* out!' When her husband, while on honeymoon, was 'putting on the dog' in Seville (in Holy Week), complaining of their poky bedroom to the management and saying: 'After all, I am the Duke of Argyll', Margaret chided him later, saying: 'Sweetie, don't try that one; in this town dukes are two-a-penny. If you want to get results, just start crackling a few crisp dollars!'

I wondered how it was that Margaret had developed, for better or for worse, into a real character. I wondered if it wasn't because for twenty-five years now she has been, and is still, a great beauty. Because of this Margaret has been in the top class; she has met interesting people. The years spent hobnobbing with Beaverbrook, millionaire Americans and English politicians, etc., have made their mark on her. Having sat next to these people for hundreds of meals, she had become a most acceptable, entertaining, companion.

I found, during this Atlantic crossing, that in her company each meal was genuinely enjoyable. Talking about the good things in life from the ivory tower of the Verandah Grill was a surprisingly pleasant way of making the journey seem short.

Part II: To and Fro, 1955-6

THE NEW COOK

London: November 1955

'What sort of meal will you have?' asks Madame Andrée, the French cook. 'A stuffed aubergine? A risotto? I can give you a magnificent dinner, of course, but a pheasant is expensive. If you have a chicken I can make it go a long way. For instance, that boiler that Mrs Beaton sent up from the country last week, with a ticket on its leg to say it was old, did very well for nine people.' It is true that the old bird appeared first with rice and cream sauce, then in some other capacity and when Ann and Laura Charteris lunched, the remains were embedded in splendid *vol-au-vents*!

Not only is Madame Andrée typically French in her parsimoniousness, but she is an artist: she can send up an egg at just the right consistency, and a salad with the perfect dressing. She is also good company. She tells me that she has broken every bone in her body, for her early years were spent performing in a circus when her crowning achievement was to be shot nightly out of a cannon.

'THE CHALK GARDEN'

New York: November

This year, instead of staying in the cushioned unreality of a luxury hotel, I rented the apartment of a Sicilian friend, Fulco Verdura: unkind friends said that in taste it was Poor Man's Charlie Bestigui. To me it was extremely pleasant, with avalanches of good art books and long-playing records of the classics; a mixture of Mannerist paintings, seventeenth- and eighteenth-century engravings, and sketches by Bérard; nice bits of china, palm trees and dark green walls, an effective if slightly sketchy attempt at interior decoration. A bell rang downstairs: a fastener on the door was a safety valve against unwelcome visitors. 'Who is it?' A voice answered my shout: 'It's the garbage man', or 'Any roaches to be got rid of?'

Even before I had unpacked I was totally engrossed with work. I was soon at such fever pitch that the servants were incredulous and said: 'Do you always keep it up like this?' Some evenings I would come back so tired that I could hardly stagger up the short flight of iron steps to my first-floor apartment, and I would fling myself on the day bed, soon to recover energy after at least three or four cups of tea from a thick, chipped-spouted, yellow earthenware teapot.

My immediate job was to assemble the furniture, props and a thousand little details for Enid Bagnold's *The Chalk Garden*. Work on this had already been going on for many months in London. It has not been an easy assignment and I would be called up late at night to talk about rethinking the whole visual conception. At weekends, too, I had to be on duty. It was not an agreeable experience, and I cannot think why I had not decided to break my contract, and be free — free — free! However, now I had more or less finished my designs, the workshops were busy building the sets and, apart from costume fittings, I was able to find time for correcting the proofs of a comic book, my experiences of a lecture tour on the blue-rinse circuit. Although the eventual possibility of production seemed more remote than ever, I also tried to do a bit of polishing to the last scene of my long-deferred

Gainsborough play. Also I did designs for a small ballet, *Soirée*, for the Met. with Karinska making the costumes.

Three whole months had gone by in an incubator of work.

It has been a Garbo-less visit. I was deeply hurt. She sent a message through Truman Capote that she wanted me to call her, that she wanted me to take her to Jamaica, but I reckoned, sadly, that she reacts more favourably to a negative reply.

THE AMBASSADOR HOTEL, NEW YORK

March 16th, 1956

Am about to return to England now that April's near. I'm told I have missed one of the most inclement winters in Europe since 1867. In fact, the cold months on Manhattan have gone by almost unnoticed, for so much of the time has been spent working indoors in artificial light that it was only when I was occasionally stranded far away from my hotel, taxiless in snowstorm or deluge, that I realised what has been happening outside.

When I arrived the sweltering heat had been like a series of blows between eyes, shoulder blades and in the solar plexus. By imperceptible degrees the temperature had dropped. Through my windows on Park Avenue a winter scene presented itself, and a pretty violent one it appeared to be but, fortunately, my work confined me to the rooms. These I have decorated myself (and for the hotel!) in a Japanese *nouveau art* manner. Since I have ceased to work for *Vogue,* I have been doing quite a lot of sittings for the deadly rival, *Harper's Bazaar.* The editor, Carmel Snow, despite all these years on the staff has never lost her innate enthusiasm and lettuce-crisp enjoyment. She is an inspiration. It gave me a new lease of life to discover the off-hand way in which she whipped up her confectionery with the slightest effort. She worked with the minimum staff, and seemed to enjoy the impromptu.

However, my main photographic work was for a book for George Weidenfeld to be called *The Face of the World*. To my strangely decorated rooms came a procession of personalities — Dr Suzuki, the great Japanese philosopher; Eudora Welty, sad and sensitive; Mary Macarthy, by whom I am determined not to be alarmed, and many other varied personages.

Jim Benton, with dark monkey-fringe for hair and a slow, deep voice, came to do a few secretarial chores for me. By degrees work became hectic, yet Jim proved himself a master-hand at keeping things under control with the ever-ringing telephone and the various chores that now kept me indoors most of the day and night. He would buy necessities for the ice-box, be messenger, look after the vastly increasing hoard of photographs which I was collecting for the book.

He gave me a perspective on the glamour potential of some of my sitters or visitors. He made, for instance, a sitting with Joan Crawford into quite an event. Very seriously he said: 'Why, she hasn't had such a distinguished workout in years!' He was less impressed by the personality of Callas, who was one of my most difficult photographic subjects. However the tornado visit of Marilyn Monroe was the greatest fun. Although one-and-a-half hours late, Marilyn was instantly forgiven for her disarming, childlike freshness, her ingenuity and irresistible mischievousness. The cupboard where the photographs were kept suddenly became full to overflowing; the bills mounted appallingly but, fortunately, so did the invoices that Jim sent out.

'MY FAIR LADY'

Working on the production of *The Chalk Garden* had been for me so deeply disturbing that I felt disinclined ever again to work for the stage as a designer. I was lucky to have had the offer of another play, which turned out to be one of the happiest productions of all time.

When that most delightful, witty and loyal of all friends, Herman Levin, had rung me in London to say Alan Lerner and Frederick Loewe were doing a musical of *Pygmalion* for him and that they wanted me for the costumes, I had not been enthusiastic about the project. Some years back the Theatre Guild had come to me with the same project. Gertie Lawrence was to be 'Eliza' and I was thrilled at such a prospect, but all had fizzled out.

There was another reason for regret: Oliver Smith had already been signed to do the scenery, and although I am devoted to Oliver, I had made a rule that I would never again participate in only one of the facets of what I considered should be a visual whole. However, I went to Claridge's and listened to Fritz Loewe strumming the music on a piano while Alan Lerner croaked his lyrics. No sooner had they given their rendering of 'The Rain in Spain stays mainly in the Plain' than I knew the venture must be a dazzling triumph. Of course I would do the costumes — better than nothing. My decision had been fortunate.

In New York I had spent five weeks working on the costumes and then returned to England where Rex Harrison's clothes were to be made. Rex is a perfectionist and demands minute attention. I had taken him to my tailor and made quick decisions about what he should wear: I work like that. If too many alternatives are suggested, I am likely to become waylaid, and even influenced for the bad. Rex is like a dog with a rat and will 'worry' details at enormous length. If given the opportunity, he will work himself up into a state of nervous alarm. I cannot say that Rex is the easiest boy in the class. But he has good taste and knows when something is not right for him. If it is wrong, he can become wild. One morning, he ripped off in anger his first-act long coat because it was tight under the arms. The seams split and the expensive stuff was frayed. The 'strait-jacket' was thrown to the floor.

But Rex is a martyr to indecisions and doubts. About this time, one evening after dinner at my house, he suddenly decided that as he had not signed his contract he did after all not wish to play the part of Henry Higgins. 'They wanted Gielgud — they'd better get him.' I telephoned in a panic to New York. Rex soon changed his mind.

One morning we had been choosing shirts, pullovers and ties in Burlington Street and, on the way to his hotel, Rex suggested I should go back with him and talk over our choice. 'It might be better if instead of the buff colour ...' He was very put out when I suddenly hailed a taxi for home.

Berman's did the right thing by the clothes that Stanley Holloway wore for Doolittle — a sweet man, gentle, unassuming and what an artist! I am ever grateful to him for giving the performance of a long lifetime.

At this time it was customary to dress almost all period musicals in the styles of the 1900s. It had become a cliché. A certain amount of opposition met the proposal that I should use the fashions of 1914 — those of the time when Shaw originally wrote the play. 'Surely they won't be sexy!' I promised they would be sexy. There was also scepticism about my idea of doing the Ascot scene in black and white. I remembered the pictures of 'Black Ascot', after King Edward

VII's death, and the effect was stunning. But for this particular scene perhaps the women would appear too much like vultures. The 'magpie' effect was the solution. Moss Hart, the director, was in agreement with me and the other chiefs shrugged their shoulders and said: 'Well, all right.'

Here at last was the opportunity to put on the stage all the memories stored up since my early boyhood. My mother's grey ostrich-feathered hat would suit Mrs Higgins at Ascot. My Bolivian Aunt Jessie's enormous cartwheel hats were remembered, and Elfie Perry, the first actress I ever met, wore a striped dress that would now be given to Eliza.

At the first reading on Broadway before the assembled company everyone was keyed up, convinced that they were participating in something exciting. Each number was spontaneously applauded. The atmosphere was electric.

I doubt if any major musical production has been brought to the stage with less difficulty. Of course it was damned hard work for all concerned, but apart from cutting a whole ballet and writing in an important scene there were the minimum of changes. Moss Hart, the captain of the crew, was brilliant, professional and tireless.

It was a happy day when Helène Pons said she would undertake to make the clothes. A dark little Russian with bruises under her eyes, a pretty mouth and a nose finely sculptured, this heroic woman worked with a sensitivity and delicacy of touch only equalled by the strength of her staying power.

Returning to New York I was now in the midst of the excitement. I was out of my hotel rooms for most of the day. (My wrist became severely strained by having to push so many times a day the heavy door of glass at the entrance of dressmaker Helène's studio building.)

Julie Andrews, an almost unknown girl who had the talent and luck to land the whopper of the part of Eliza, was almost unbelievably naive and simple. She was angelically patient at the many fittings of her clothes and never expressed an opinion. One day, due to exhaustion at rehearsals, she keeled over in a dead faint while fitting her resplendent ball gown. A Dixie cup of cold water was enough to revive her and she reproached herself that her mother, back home in Walton-on-Thames, would be ashamed of her. 'Oh, Mummie, what a silly girl I am,' she kept repeating.

One evening when we had seen enough of Julie's performance to know that she was absolutely perfect for the role, I rather impertinently said that she must try always to remember this most wonderful moment in her career, when she was just about to burst on the world as a star. It was typical of Julie's modesty and professionalism to say in a somewhat Eliza-like phrase: 'The only thing that matters is if I do it right.' She did!

Nothing could have been more exquisite than Cathleen Nesbitt's little cameo as Mrs Higgins and she never suggested for a moment that I had overdressed her. Bob Coote was totally effective as the waffling Colonel Pickering.

Rex Harrison was by now extremely tense; never having appeared in a musical before, and doing something so utterly different, he felt he could not rehearse enough. The chorus-girls, long since exhausted, lay on the floor or were sprawled in the stalls, while Rex repeated, over and over again, certain phrases of 'I've grown accustomed to her face'. At length, when he was playing the last-act fight scene with Liza and she threw the slippers hard in his face, the entire chorus applauded from the stalls.

No doubt Rex was right. He knew his performance was more important than the impatience of thirty chorus-girls and dancers. However, Rex's continuing egotism upset me to such an extent that only by a miracle was I prevented from making an ugly scene. I was so steamed up to fury on some now forgotten account, and was just about to burst into his room to tell him what I thought of him — an idiotic, pointless and impertinent thing to do in any case — when I was interrupted by the stage manager: 'Moss wants you immediately at the back of the stalls.'

The dress rehearsals in Newhaven were long-drawn-out and complicated. Yet the unions did not prevent their continuing until near dawn. By dint of Moss' brilliant organising and with help from the stage manager, Bud, the show was able to open in extremely smooth shape.

The news of the success of *My Fair Lady*, as *Pygmalion* was at last named, spread from Newhaven to New York. I had never before worked for a big Broadway musical and I only now realised what it meant to participate in a grand opening.

The performance of the first night audience was as brilliant as that on the stage. Every joke was appreciated, every nuance enjoyed and the various numbers were received with thunder-claps. The success was beyond all expectation. I did not understand how great it was until next day, while sauntering up Park Avenue. I came across someone whom I knew very little for he had never seemed to acknowledge my existence. I was, therefore, extremely surprised when he said: 'Hullo Seesil, good to see you. You really are quite a guy!'

Success on such a scale now seemed easy, and I wondered why it had never happened before. It had taken such a long time to achieve. It had not come too late, yet I was, perhaps, a bit bitter that some of my friends in the theatre (if there is such an anomaly) did not have confidence in my talent twenty years before. Nonetheless it was pleasant to enjoy it now.

On the last lap of my stay a snowstorm blanketed New York, and its commuters were isolated. Everything at a standstill for two days; appointments cancelled; I had to delay my sailing by a week. In this time I was able to squeeze in most of the pressing urgencies, including the designing of a set of modern clothes, based on *My Fair Lady*, for a Seventh Avenue wholesale firm.

The telephone seldom stopped ringing, and messengers arrived with packages, or people arrived by appointment. Now the various jobs of work are finished. There are no visible signs of spring in Central Park but those definite vibrations are in the air. I'm impatient to get home, and to see what, in my garden, has survived the great frost.

The last three days were the worst. The rooms were turned upside down as packing started. But, harassing as it was, we were all buoyed up by the fact that things were going well. The faithful Margaret Case went with me to get my exit permit. Jim promised he would pack any belongings that were left behind once I had gone off to the boat. I arrived at the dock too late for any further visitors to come aboard. I waved to Margaret and Jim and others who had appeared. Hooting — an eerie sound. I went to my cabin and I lay on the bunk. I felt I was on the crest of a wave and must enjoy the ride.

It was rather a shock to realise that I had been away from my home for almost seven months out of eight. Those months had been creative. I was not displeased with my efforts. It had been a time without particularly irksome love troubles or lack of love. I had never allowed myself to get beyond a certain pitch of exhaustion, and it seemed that my stars were favourably disposed. Things that seemed to have developed slowly in recent years suddenly came to fruition.

GRETA

New York

Our last meeting had ended on a high emotional note. The scene had taken place in her rather too ornate apartment. I had drunk vodka cocktails. When Greta mentioned a twenty-year-old score-something about her having no heart I became uncontrollably angry. 'If after all these years you can't forget that, then I'm a failure and our friendship means nothing!'

I banged out of the apartment. She came to the elevator to stop me. 'Then you won't marry me?' she joked. But it was no joke to me.

When I had got back to England I wrote her one long, serious, sad letter. Then I decided on silence. When I came back to New York I did not call her. I did not answer her messages sent through Truman. I went home again and I still did not write.

On my return to New York I waited before telephoning her. She was contrite and sweet. We were friends again, and yet the relationship was different. I had consciously put a brake on my emotions.

One day she telephoned me: 'I believe we're both going to lunch at Madame de Becker's?' 'Yes, shall we go there together,' I asked, 'or shall we go under our own steam?' 'Our own steam is better.' She had particular reasons for not wanting us to be seen arriving together.

Greta looked a bit shiny-faced and palely beautiful in a grey dress. But I was determined to remain untouched by her beauty. While having coffee after lunch the conversation centred around works of art, and our hostess said: 'Greta, you're the only one "up". Go and fetch the *Connaissance des Arts* from the next room.' Greta, the Empress, looked aghast at being spoken to in this peremptory manner, and then she half-saved the situation by doing an extremely comic imitation of a drunkard reeling out of the room.

Later, 'by appointment', Greta came to my hotel on the dot. I was as bright and gay as I could be, but the spirit had died in me. Greta is an extremely intuitive person; it was obvious that sensing this, she became ill-at-ease and worried. When the time came for her to leave, she turned and waved to me down the corridor with a sweet, sad expression on her face that broke my heart. When I telephoned to her a few days later, she said: 'I never thought, after our last meeting, that you'd ever call me again.'

I did not want to cut off our friendship, but the flame of my love had been dampened down on purpose by me. Determinedly I became engrossed in my work. The calendar each week became a fretwork of interlocking dates. If I rang and asked Greta to dine next Friday, she would be incapable of giving an answer until the last minute. So I saw little of her, and whenever I telephoned, it was just a question of 'keeping in touch'.

Jakie Astor, one of my nicest and most amusing friends, arrived in New York. He wanted to meet Greta and, after a certain amount of prevarication, she decided to come to a small dinner I was to give. At the last moment she rang up to know if I really expected her. (She had already decided to come with Cecile Rothschild.) Well then, was it all right if she wore trousers? She arrived in grey with a turban on her head. She had made the minimum effort, but this was enough to make her outstanding. She seemed dazzling in her own luminous light, spellbound and spellbinding. Her eyes melted and showed that the old feeling was still there. I capitulated. It was lovely to feel in love with her again, to be enveloped in a tender cocoon of an emotion after wearing the hairshirt of self-defence.

From this evening our telephone conversations became friendly and jocose again. Even so, we didn't meet much. Then her health became bad. She could not say what was the matter; she had been to the Medical Centre for tests each day. She talked with terrible foreboding on the telephone: she moaned, felt ill, could do nothing, and went out very little.

When I went to see her, she told me that the doctors had found out that the matter with her was not serious and that she would recover. She exclaimed: 'The relief! The joy! Because, although I do nothing, go nowhere, and lead an empty life, yet I love every minute of it! I'm never bored! Only there's never enough time! I'm in my room pottering about. Two hours have gone by, then a whole day! Sometimes I wake up in the middle of the night, and I can't believe that I'm no longer leading the sort of life I used to — that I'm no longer making motion pictures — that all is over. I can't think where the time has gone.'

On the day before I was sailing, we lunched together at our accustomed table. Unfortunately, I had to leave directly after to pay my taxes, and she had to go to the hospital, so that our shopping expedition was not possible. I watched her out of the taxi window as she walked down the street. She looked sad and pale, her skin crinkled and papery, and there was a shiny residue of cold cream around her eyes. The tax man only took a second to get my signature, and I thought maybe I could find Greta again on Lexington Avenue, but she had disappeared.

That evening I went to say goodbye to her in her apartment. 'Life is such a compromise! I wanted to live in such a different place from this, and yet one must have tables and chairs! But these are not what I like.' Only her almost unfurnished dining room, where there is a great, solid table that could have been Queen Christina's, looks as if it belonged to her. The ormulu, the bound volumes (never opened), the bits of china were all bought under the influence of the 'little man'.

We talked of plans for meeting in Europe during the summer — all very indefinite. The time was coming for me to leave. I had once wanted to talk to her about our 'row', to 'clear the atmosphere', but the opportunity did not come; I was rather pleased that it did not. We were now on terms of easy intimacy; why spoil anything so pleasant?

But suddenly she said that she had been wanting to answer my 'serious' letter. She had wanted to say: 'I do love you, and I think you're a flop! You should have taken me by the scruff of my neck and made an honest boy of me. I think you could have been the Salvation Army.' 'Thank you for telling me that,' I murmured.

I had much to think about on my way down in the elevator, and in the street, and on my way to dinner. I would have much to think about later on the boat. Maybe it was not too late, after all, to try and recapture the past? Maybe life did hold new possibilities now that the stars seemed to be under good aspect?

PETER WATSON

Sunday, May 6th

I lunched with Peter at a branch of Wheeler's restaurant that is near to his Institute of Contemporary Arts in Dover Street.

Peter was busy hanging an exhibition of garden schemes from Brazil and could not spare time off to get back to my house for lunch.

We talked, as always, very animatedly. He had survived the rigours of winter though he had been feeling terribly ill and had gone to my Dr Gottfried. He spoke with such gusto and intelligence that I was very happy to listen and admire his point of view; his ever-sensitive appreciation for so many aspects of art and life. I thought that he was a completely fulfilled, integrated person; someone who has been through many vicissitudes and has now discovered himself.

Peter is an independent, courageous person, on terms of absolute honesty with himself, with the world, and with everybody he talks to.

Tony del Renzio, whom I had seen with Peter at the ICA a few days ago, telephoned. I let out a moan that was like that of a bull in agony. I could not speak and I asked him to wait until I had given myself fresh energy to face the dreadful fact that Peter was dead.

Nearly thirty years I have known Peter ... here a painting of Ashcombe we had found together — so many books — so many memories — snapshots taken in every part of the world — America, Mexico, Austria, Germany, France. I dressed like Peter and I behaved like him.

Later he wore awful mackintoshes — his hair, once so sexily lotioned, was on end. He was a real bohemian — gone the elegant clothes and motorcars. He had become thinner and more gaunt and of a bad colour.

He had edited *Horizon* with Cyril Connolly and become a serious art patron in a quiet, unobtrusive way. He was deeply interested in music, painting, sculpture and poetry. He read books in many languages, and thought a great deal about politics. He was intensely single-minded. Sometimes I would watch him as he talked with such concentration and he would look like a ruffled old chicken, his complexion yellow; he had become very sloppy about shaving and generally had a few cuts around the face. But however awful he looked, he had a quality of beauty. He relied less and less on charm; but his smile was so disarming that people could not but like him.

PETER'S FUNERAL

May

The coffin was totally against his taste; the red brick chapel and all the details of the service were the sort of things Peter would have no patience for.

Among the congregation, with its trustees, lawyers and family business associates, it was difficult to identify Peter's friends. Norman was high up in the front pews, very quiet and imaginative; Stephen S. and his wife; Lee Miller and her husband, Roland Penrose; Reid, the picture dealer; Tony del Renzio. The service was meaningless to me in my hollow state of mind. I noticed that Cyril Connolly was weeping and I loved him for that; but from my seat in the back of the church I could not see or hear or feel anything but anonymity.

It was a cold, horrid afternoon. The chapel door was open and gusts of gritty wind gushed from the asphalt outside. The clergyman hurried through the service in double-quick time, and the appalling moment came when the metal doors opened on their mechanical hinges and the coffin slowly moved forth on a conveyor belt to the other world. I was strangely unmoved and watched the trembling flowers going through to the outer space. Suddenly a ray of brilliant sunshine came down onto the flowers. It was a most dramatic and beautiful effect — the lilies became incandescent in this drab, horrible surrounding. I almost believed that this symbol meant that Peter had attained a happiness that was denied him on this earth, and it helped me to think that he might be in a state of serenity after his turbulent years.

I went to the car park and the clipped voice of Mr Brewer said: 'They don't take long in getting through with it, do they!' A quarter-of-an-hour had passed since we had turned into the red brick gateway — a quarter of a century's friendship had been 'written off'.

VISIT TO CHANEL IN PARIS

Chanel has been the most important influence on fashion since the 1914 war. The young girl of peasant stock had come from the Auvergne where she had been spotted by the elderly Etienne Balsan, who brought her to Deauville and set her up as a milliner. At once her hats were successful, but the grand and respectable ladies frequented her emporium only in the mornings, for too many men were to be found there in the afternoon. Under the influence of the Grand Duke Dmitri she added to her knowledge of the best in French and Czarist Russian taste. Later she came under the protection of Boy Capell, a man of exceptional flair who proved to be perhaps the love of her life. But Boy Capell died young in a motor crash, and Chanel's protectors then became numerous. She learnt a great deal from them all.

From millinery Chanel progressed to dresses. She made Russian blouses and skirts, and used English tweeds and jerseys. When she opened a shop in Paris she gave rich women the 'poor' look that made her fortune. Chanel herself was the embodiment of the new 'chic': flat-chested, devastatingly attractive, with a boy's hips, long thin legs in her 'kasha' colour suits and cropped black hair.

Her successes continued. Her romance with the rich Duke of Westminster became notorious. The duke gave her a block of property in Mayfair, a mill where she designed her particular brand of English tweeds, and a gold-mine in jewels; she was seen in the hunting field with rows of pearls swinging on her habit. Her temperamental scenes and extravagances were violent. It was said that Chanel was the one woman who was never sycophantic or subservient to this incredibly spoilt man. He gave in to her every whim, even setting up a workroom for her at Eaton Hall, complete with her French staff, rather than have her return to Paris a month earlier to make her season's collection. When she was displeased, and the duke tried to placate her with offerings of jewellery, she was likely to stamp on them or throw them through the porthole of his yacht.

Her business continued to prosper with each year. Then came World War II. France under the Occupation became a prison; fashion dead.

Now, after an interval of fourteen years, French friends and acquaintances seemed vague about whether or not Chanel still existed. They had positively no idea of her whereabouts since, during the war, she had taken a good-looking husky German as a lover. Certainly, she had long since given up making clothes; the windows in the Rue Cambon still displayed bottles of '*Numéro Cinq*'. However, it was not really difficult to discover that the 'pariah' was still to be found in the apartment at the top of her dress shop. She would be delighted to see me.

Paris seemed empty during that weekend. It was almost an uncanny experience to enter the deserted Chanel building, to walk past row upon row of display stalls long since covered with dust sheets, then up flight after flight of the mirrored stairs, eventually to arrive at a door that opened onto her private apartment and into an Aladdin's cave of oriental splendour; an unbelievable richness of Venetian glass mirrors reflecting lacquer screens, gesso tables and Tang horses.

Strains of Wagner wafted from a hidden gramophone through the expensively scented atmosphere. An eminent-looking businessman, with a folio of papers under his arm, greeted me in whispers, and in pantomime invited me to accompany him. 'Come here quick, quick!' With a magician's gesture, he bid me behold: '*Voilà!*' Chanel was asleep on an enormous suede sofa. She was fully dressed, wearing a hat, with a sable rug thrown over her; she had assumed a pose of graceful abandon.

But I felt guilty that I had intruded. It was as if I were looking at someone dead; so, after a moment of admiration, I retreated to the hall while the businessman decided to wake her. Moments later the 'outcast' rushed from the corridor to greet me. It was as if a whole box of fireworks had suddenly gone off: splutters of squibs, diamonds from sparklers, pops from jumping Jacks, and even the whoosh of a rocket. Chanel was talking, laughing, gesticulating, grimacing — in fact, being herself.

After the first pyrotechnic onslaught had successfully won the audience to her side, I realised what a strange and extraordinary sight presented itself: a sunburnt old gipsy was thrusting her unbelievably raddled face within an inch of my nose. One could see that her cheeks had been pulled up to the ears by a violent surgeon, and there were deep lines from the great gash of her almost lipless mouth to the incredibly wide nostrils of her toadstool nose.

The flashing smile and over-brimming vitality soon became hypnotic; the darting blackbird eyes were never still; the rich, creamy croak from deep down her larynx was urgent, confidential, conspiratorial. This *jolie laide* still played her games of attraction expertly. Her welcome was so warm and spontaneous that I felt I had regained a long-lost relation.

Wearing a buff-coloured coat and skirt trimmed with leopard skin, Chanel had arrived years ago in my mother's drawing room to be one of my first professional sitters. I was easily alarmed by strangers, and found her particularly difficult to approach. When, years later, she came to New York, and appeared as the very quintessence of Parisian chic at a candle-lit supper party given by the dressmaker, Charles James, she was overwhelmingly attractive, but she seemed to swat her admirers as if they were so many obtrusive flies. How different the reception today!

Back in the sitting room I now had the opportunity to scrutinise a little the Golconda collection: the crystal chandeliers, Chinese screens and tables, life-size gilded gazelles and antelopes, the gold objects, the precious stone animals, so typically mixed with classical Greek statues, Italian carvings and Japanese junk. Chanel apologised that the flat was not finished, that no curtains were hanging at the tall window; but, nevertheless, she preferred living in unfurnished rooms. 'It gives a feeling of life — vitality.' She likes her things to be put around in an impromptu manner; nothing to be arranged or set.

Although she has not designed clothes for many years she appeared today to be ahead of fashion, so incredibly spruce she was, in a Beau Brummel way — yet totally French in navy blue serge over white linen blouse. Every detail was of an exquisite refinement and immaculate quality. The simplicity of her perfectly tailored suit was paradoxically overwhelmed by a fantastic array of jewels: strings of pearls hanging in cascades among chains of rubies and emeralds and gold links around her incredibly thin, stringy neck, and her mushroom hat and a lapel of her coat were each adorned with a vast sunburst of diamonds.

Her appeal for friendliness, her frank lack of reserve, her wide-apart legs with continual flexing of knees, gave one the impression of an attractive young schoolboy, and yet her grace and appeal are entirely feminine. Her hands, without nail varnish, are a young girl's hands and the skin is satiny and unwrinkled.

In her deep, gruff, catarrhal monotone she jabbered non-stop, but it was up to me to try to dam the torrent and start work on the drawing for my book. Her enthusiasm was untiring. Such vitality is irresistible; I could well see why so many remarkable men and women had found her devastating.

Suddenly she asked if her talk was distracting for me. 'Yes, a bit,' I had to admit, for my drawing was progressing badly. At last a wonderful silence ensued. The face I peered at was defiant, courageous, alert and tragic. There was no apology for its wear and tear, or for the almost shocking brutality of the down-thrusted sledge-hammer of a mouth.

Chanel had nothing to do. Now that she wasn't working she had leisure. She was living the life she'd always been unable to live; at last she could meet young people, travel and read; she realised, a little, what was going on in the world. She protested perhaps too much that one must not think of the past, but become part of the changed world. She complained of bores, and was disloyal to her old friends, Maggie Van Zuylen and Cocteau; she denounced the recent 'old hat' exhibition of Dali. *Apropos* of fashion, she said that it had died with the last war and no longer existed or had become entirely commercial: 'Fashion is now in the hands of American Seventh Avenue and the pederasts.'

It is unattractive when older people are poisonous about their rivals. Chanel pronounced opinions that most other women would not have dared to voice. Yet somehow one could not believe in her display of hatred and jealousy; it was as if she were acting the words without feeling. A lot of conversation was geared to the fact that she wished to rehabilitate herself in the eyes of the very Parisians she despised and who, because of her 'collabo' reputation, had dropped her cold. There was an extra reason why she should put herself in a good light for me. She was far too subtle to mention the subject of her 'disgrace', but it was important that she should get word through to Winston Churchill to tell him what a lot she had done for England. Churchill had known her in the South of France before the war; but recently he had not replied to her letters, and it was vital that the British Embassy here in Paris should see to it that he received her messages. Would I say something to Duff Cooper?

My drawings drove me to despair: my energy had become so dispersed that the ink line had no strength behind it. I would come back again tomorrow — and so the long first session came to an end.

Being in Chanel's company was like a strange journey into the past. Without interruptions from friends, or from telephone calls, it was as if I had spent an afternoon with a character from history. The result was not a disappointment for, whatever her faults, she was unique.

BERTIE ABDY

It is doubtful whether anyone will write a life of that most retiring of men, Bertie Abdy, for he has always courted anonymity and would certainly give no active help to his biographer; in fact, he would be as uncooperative, stubborn and difficult as only he knows how to be. Bertie's lack of compromise has reduced his list of friends to the minimum. To a very carefully sifted little group, who love him for his peculiarities, Bertie has always been irresistible.

Although his father disliked anything connected with the arts, Bertie became passionately interested at the age of ten in the aesthetic world. Later, when he inherited his fantastic fortune (he owned a large slice of the London Docks), he was able to cultivate his ambition to almost unlimited lengths. He denigrates his penchant for the pretty: 'I suppose everything I like is "chocolate-boxy", but look at this Fragonard — isn't it lovely! Every rose bush a Cadbury!' Yet he is surprisingly catholic in his tastes; he is a collector of Renaissance bronzes and was among the first to introduce to London such painters as Degas and Kokoschka. But when even Bertie could not afford to buy more statuary, paintings, books or *objets* for himself, he bought for others. He became expert in advising Chester Beatty, Gulbenkian and other rich collectors in the world. When most of his dockland property was destroyed by fire, he went into business to the extent of advising and finding rare items for such firms as Wildenstein, Seligmann and Partridge.

Bertie is incapable of being a shrewd businessman and feathering his own nest. The essence of integrity himself, he is never embittered when tricked by crooked agents. But his honesty and his lack of tact have made him many enemies.

One of his usual sallies is to give advice that is not welcome. Once I showed him a painting of mine that had gone wrong. He told me that there was nothing to be done but fly immediately to Spain to see how Goya would have tackled the problem in an entirely different way. Few people relish his outspokenness. He called Sir Joseph Duveen a mountebank; and when Mrs Neeley Vanderbilt showed him her Fifth Avenue house and explained: 'This is the *Louis Seize* drawing-room', Bertie asked: 'And what makes you think it is?' On another occasion a Chilean friend, Tony Gandarillas, bewailing the fact that his elderly dog had become frail and possibly could not live much longer, said he would like to take him to Brighton to see the sea before he died. Bertie enquired: 'Wouldn't it be better if you took the dog to the Wallace Collection?'

Bertie's standards are so high that he even designated the Kent furniture made specially for the Double Cube Room at Wilton as 'so coarse, it'd be all right for a circus roundabout'. He dismissed the taste of the interior decorator Elsie de Wolfe as 'ribbons and rubbish'.

I have come to stay with Bertie in his rough-hewn stone house, Newton Ferrers, in Cornwall. A catastrophic fire gutted one whole wing that contained many of his greatest treasures; nonetheless, in other parts of the house a collection of rare books, pictures and sculptures remains unscathed, and the garages, stables, and other out-houses are still filled with terracottas, old-master drawings and Boulle furniture, which he cannot bear to sell.

Bertie, blinking through huge tortoiseshell-rimmed glasses, climbs a step-ladder in his library and hands down a slim volume to be admired. 'What could be prettier than this binding with the Bourbon arms, 1753? Look at this — no one in England ever did anything to equal this sort of thing!' His long, white, cheese-stick fingers falter along the tops of gold-tooled volumes. 'This is a pretty book for wig-makers and hairdressers of the eighteenth century.' His voice seems even sadder. 'Now this beautiful binding just shows how civilised they were to honour a book on how to make two hundred and fifty different *meringues*! This machinery is for blowing the icing sugar.' A few steps higher on the ladder and Bertie points out the calligraphy of the Dauphin's prayer book. 'Madame de Behargue offered me a thousand pounds for this! I bought it in London for a song. Ah, but mine's only a child's collection!' moans Bertie, coming down the ladder and thinking of the things he would have liked to buy.

Then, unexpectedly, Bertie's face breaks into a thousand pieces as he laughs, takes off his spectacles to polish them with his handkerchief, and explains: 'I'm so hard up I can't afford to go to London any more.' His face becomes ashen and grave again. 'Eleven shillings for a meal — it's preposterous! And uneatable too! That's why I go to Lyon's for a bun and a cup of milk.'

I have the feeling that if Bertie were to become a pauper, he would somehow continue never to lower his standards of perfection; he would always insist on only the best quality. Today he considers that he leads a squalid, slum-like existence. Anything less ordinary cannot be imagined than Bertie, gaunt, myopic and papyrus-complexioned, sitting in an exquisite Jacob chair, flicking expertly through a catalogue, while his lanky legs sprawl for miles over the Savonnerie carpet until they end in a pair of elephantine bedroom slippers. Bertie points at a rare Provencal commode saying: 'I must get rid of this absurd rusticity.'

'You can't find anyone to do anything for you nowadays. I used to travel a lot to see dealers and works of art. I'm not a manager, and I don't know how to look after myself. Edwards, my man, used to do everything. I don't care if he stank of my sherry — he looked after me. I'd say: "Get me to Brussels" and he'd manage it. Once, going to Vienna, I found myself on the wrong train; Edwards realised it, and somehow he got on to it and fetched me back. Edwards had a sense of the art of living. He enjoyed his work. He'd spend hours boning my boots. Who has his boots boned today? And each time I put on my clothes they had been ironed — underclothes and pyjamas always ironed! And that man did all the silver! Have you ever tried to clean silver? And the porcelain — every bit he had to wash himself. I used to give Edwards tips — a cheque for one hundred pounds if business was good, and fifty pounds at Christmas. When he left I gave him five hundred pounds because he was worth it.'

At Newton Ferrers today there is no one to valet Bertie (he wears old gamekeeper's clothes during the day and green velvet suits at night). He still orders a thousand more flowering cherry trees to blossom in his 'suburban garden of pink veils' ('a million cherry trees and never a cherry'), and once a month he can't resist buying, however small, a Fragonard or a Rouault.

Bertie admits that the new world which has taken charge baffles him. 'It's so entirely different! When I went to fight the Second War I didn't understand what they were talking about, it was a new language. The first time someone said "Cheerio" I was absolutely dumbfounded. But there are no manners any more, and no officer is looked after as he used to be. In the First War we had batmen and they wore livery in the evening: we had old silver on the table. Now the squalor! The bathrooms are dirty, the water closets are poisonous. Everyone drinks beer, and the noise! And I'm talking about a great regiment! One that is entitled to wear the King's livery — with silk stockings and buckles.' Yet Bertie is deep in homage to the discipline and courage of the Brigade of Guards. 'When the country was trying to exist and facing destruction, the men were behaving like mythological heroes, literally fighting to the last man. They considered it was a privilege to die.'

When reality in the form of today's ruthlessness and lack of manners encroaches uncomfortably near Bertie, we discover someone who will not submit without a fight. This most sensitive soul has a white-hot temper and often his scorn brings a healthy *volte-face* to a bully. However, travelling with Bertie can make one blush with shame. At Waterloo Station he was abruptly stopped at the barrier by a policeman putting an arm across his chest, and shouting at him to join the queue for the platform. Bertie, a towering Peter Schlemiel emitting electric sparks of rage, bellowed: 'I haven't fought the Germans to be told by someone like you to join a queue. I'll strike you first with my umbrella before I join that queue!' 'I suppose you're a gentleman!' sneered the policeman. 'I'm English,' yelled Bertie and so great was the force of his fury that he was allowed past the barriers onto the train.

Once in the railway carriage he settled down to talk about Horace or the merits of wine. The doors open. In a stage whisper Bertie moans: 'Oh, two more women with unwashed hair!'

Tonight at dinner Bertie talked about life in Paris between the two wars. 'Madame de Behargue spent all her life looking for a certain object. She found that carafe over there that she had been wanting for thirty years — and she found it three months before she died.'

He continued: 'It's extraordinary what England has been through! At the time of Charles II the rich people were living on porridge.' He then reminisced with regret: 'No one knows wine any more, no one appreciates good food, no one knows anything about art.'

HENRY MOORE

One of Bertie Abdy's most recent possessions is a bronze torso by Henry Moore. This piece of sculpture has been very much in the news. It is said to have been inspired by Moore's first visit to Greece and is considered a work of importance. In fact the Directors of the Manchester Art Museum were interested in buying it, but at the last moment the voting went against them, resulting in newspaper headlines and controversies. The piece has now been placed temporarily by Bertie at Newton Ferrers in Cornwall in a position dominating his elaborately cascading water garden. Henry Moore was due, at any moment, to give his advice about where best it should be permanently placed.

Out of the local taxi bundled hurriedly a little businessman in rough tweeds with a North Country accent. He had, I thought, a rather anonymous appearance; plain pudding-face, weak eyes, pale blue, watery but bright, a beaky nose and irregular, somewhat parrot-beak teeth and a high forehead with receding hair laid flat and lifeless across the dome. No time to be lost before taking him down to the water garden to try and find Bertie. He talked in staccato, jerky sentences and struck his words with insistent hammer-force. He seemed to be trying to overcome an innate nervousness and shyness (and I too).

It took us both a few moments to realise that we shared that particular fraternity of feeling that is common to most people who practise in the world of the arts; we were soon talking as if we had known one another of old.

But if I felt Moore and I had struck a chord of sympathy, it was nothing to the soaring harmony of understanding and genuine recognition that was sparked off the moment that Henry Moore met Bertie. Henry Moore became immediately and completely at ease; Bertie, whose views are not readily understood by many who are practising artists, found at once that he had a soul-mate.

Bertie showed the sculptor the possible sites from which the figure could be seen at good advantage. The three of us marched up, down and around beside the cascades. Finally Henry Moore was convinced that the site chosen by Bertie, at the fount of the water display, was the most effective. We celebrated the decision.

On Sunday morning the sun shone on the newly budding trees, on the primroses and on Bertie's thousand cherries. A Cornish spring was beginning in earnest. Bertie, with leisure such as few are able to possess today, had already done some work in the woods with his cutter, had played a game of croquet with his son, Valentine, and now bid me come for a walk with him.

We found Henry Moore and set off. In the spring woods the bluebells were beginning: everywhere was joy. Bertie and Henry talked about works of art and of the great masters as if they were intimate friends. 'No,' said Bertie, 'I don't think money is necessarily a deterrent to creativity. Degas was rich; Cézanne was well off. In fact, very few of the Impressionists were poor. But happiness, without the contrasting periods of misery, is not good for an artist. We must all endure a certain hell within us; Michelangelo's suffering — his appalling torments of jealousy for his young men — surely stimulated his imagination.'

These two new friends bubbled with such enthusiasm and brimmed over with so much information that I suffered an acute bout of inferiority. Why hadn't I been informing myself all these years on the subjects that are close to me? How was it that I did not possess the power of enjoying and enthusing as they could? I felt doltish and hidebound.

It often gives one a sea change to be in the presence of a highly individual artist for suddenly one can see the world through his eyes. To be with Dali is to discover that the fire-irons are strange surrealist spiders; in the company of Jean Cocteau one finds that almost everywhere, even in the most prosaic surroundings, there are curious neoromantic phenomena. On this walk one suddenly saw Henry Moore bowls and holes in the thick trunks of trees; the trees themselves became like Moore figures. Once or twice the sculptor leant down to pick up a small gnarled root or a stone with a striking shape that interested him sufficiently to put in his pocket and preserve for possible future use.

Determined not to be left out of the party, though very much in third place, I at last broached my subject. 'How and when did you decide to become a sculptor?' The answer was pat. 'When I was a small boy, living with my family in a small mining town, twenty thousand population, Castleford in Yorkshire. I was the seventh of eight children. We were sometimes sent off on Sunday afternoons to listen to some lecture at the school house. The main purpose was really to give us something to do, keep us away from our home, and allow the parents a bit of a rest. One Sunday someone told me a story about Michelangelo who was carving a figure of an old fawn, and a local farmer's lad who came along to watch him at work. After a few minutes the lad commented that so old an animal would not have all its teeth intact — whereupon Michelangelo took the chisel and knocked out a few teeth.' The point of the story was to show that even the greatest can learn something from the simplest; but for Henry Moore the story was important for, having heard it, he knew somehow that he wanted to be a sculptor. From that moment on, whenever asked, 'tinker, tailor' fashion, what he wished to be in life he always piped up 'sculptor'. Fortunately he was sent to Castleford Secondary School which was run by a remarkable man whose ideas of education were so unconventional and imaginative that the parents and the Board of Governors were always fighting him and trying to get him sacked. They disliked the way that suddenly all lessons would be stopped, and the whole school would assemble to listen to classical music. One day the young Henry Moore was whistling an air of Mozart as he went down a corridor. The headmaster rushed out at him. 'Whistle that again,' he commanded. The little Moore was then made to whistle the piece to the whole school, to prove a point.

A wonderful woman, half-English, half-French, the art mistress (Alice Gosdick), showed little Henry the *Studio* magazines, and the 'arty-crafty', art-decorative pictures fashionable at that time (1911). These set the fuse to work, and he became more than ever determined to sculpt. Miss Gosdick gave Moore his first job of carving (the School Roll of Honour).

As we walked up steep hills, past cottages made of the local grey stone, the talk passed on to other more diversified subjects. Among the opinions expressed by Bertie was that there should be a tax on illegitimate babies, a tax on a third child and a heavy fine for venereal disease; there should be public brothels, all women forced to wear a pessary, and certainly the laws on homosexuality relaxed and made civilised enough for us not to be the laughing stock of other countries. Bertie also opined that no one could understand works of art if they had only eaten filthy food and had no taste for wine. He was inspired to be his most exaggerated self, the acme of refinement, Olympian, perhaps a bit decadent, a far cry indeed from Henry Moore, whose face was becoming quite pink as he hurried along to keep up with Bertie's enormous strides. Although Henry could not quite agree with some of Bertie's more high-flown fantasies, the two of them were fundamentally in agreement. Art has no barriers and these two figures, in their diversified ways, are both artists.

Bertie, always diffident about showing his works of art to others and deprecating his possessions, was fired by Henry Moore's enthusiasm to bring out all sorts of objects that perhaps even he had forgotten. Henry did not seem to light up at the sight of some early classical fragments, his John of Bologna, or even his prize Donatello. Henry dismissed the Pajou and Carpeaux, and only when he saw the Rodins did he burn with genuine enthusiasm. Bertie wondered why modern sculptors ignore the past: 'Most of them are really only interested in the sexual organs, and they're so terribly boring!' Henry laughed loudly.

The weekend continued in a most effervescing spirit of camaraderie. Henry played croquet wearing a ridiculous hat. We visited a strange pile of monolithic stones dating, it is said, from two thousand years before Christ. The stones are of such mammoth size that one cannot imagine how primitive man placed them one on top of the other; an impressive place. We looked at a variety of works of art *chez* neighbouring Norman Colville (drawings of Fra Angelico, Tintoretto, Michelangelo, sculpture by Verrocchio, etc.). We drank champagne and acted ridiculous charades, in which Henry was at first somewhat backward but soon warmed to the game. Later he became extremely funny when acting out the word 'enthusiastic', and gushed: 'Oh, I do *so* love sculpture! I just *adore* going out into my studio and, taking my chisel and hammer, going "bang! bang bang!"'

In the railway carriage on our way home we kept up continuous conversation. Henry was unable to contain his enthusiasm for the beauties of the springtime landscapes of Somerset. He kept jumping to his feet to point out as it rolled by some particular vista or phenomenon bathed in blue mists.

Henry considered carving to be soothing work, not too strenuous either physically or mentally. It was more exciting than digging in the garden, but not so exhausting. Much of the time the work was automatic; he could work for eight or twelve hours a day. But drawing, or inventing new shapes in small model form, was creative and took a greater toll.

By the time the train had arrived at Salisbury, where I had to leave the party, I noticed how Henry's face had quite transcended its contours. It had become lively and sparkling, rippling with laughter, the hair blown into a natural shape, the mouth no longer parrot-like. A complete transformation had overcome the rather steely façade that he had presented on his hurried descent from the local taxi.

Part III: Far Eastern Adventure, 1957

January 1957

Two days after Christmas, Truman Capote and I set off on our expedition. Truman never slogs on after he's tired; he says no when he has had enough and evaporates from a conversation that bores him. He has complete knowledge of himself and his limitations, and is a totally integrated human being. He says: 'I've got the exact formula. I've worked it all out.' Whether it be his capacity for drink, his feelings about loves, friends, acquaintances, or strangers, he knows what he is about.

Truman can remember facts, dates, sums of money with an uncanny sharpness. Someone can hold forth about the economic situation, and three days later he can repeat it word for word. His powers of concentration are greater than any I've known; he is interested in many aspects of life, and has a great sense of humour. Above all, he is a marvellous travelling companion.

On the aeroplane to Honolulu the stewards giggled a lot, showing rows of excellent teeth. They were lanky and lean, their complexions poreless and magnolia-textured. The stewardesses were extremely pretty in a delicate, doll-like way. They served us with circles of white rice with black fish-skin sprinkled with pink and green crystals, and raw fish covered in batter.

Leis of carnations, ginger, tuberoses and orchids were put round our necks when we landed on this island on a breezeless evening. The palm trees were motionless, and birds with very small heads were twittering in the branches.

The sky was blue, the sea a paler blue. The people have a beauty that is so perfect that there is little sex appeal, and they all wear clothes of brilliant colours — scarlet, scarlet and white, scarlet and yellow.

It is the ideal climate; throughout the year it changes only twelve degrees.

KAUAI

The island, half an hour from Hawaii, looked very beautiful as it sped by the car windows in a pink fluff of swaying, sugarcane tassels. The wind blew hard and the sun shone on the tassels and made them appear of spun silk. Pineapples, growing in strict formation, created a very sophisticated colour effect.

Robert Allerton, 85, a rich farmer formerly of Illinois, with his friend, John Grieg, an architect, disciple of David Adler, discovered this little house, once lived in by Queen Emma, at the foot of a mountain range. It is at the water's edge, where a river runs into a blue sea. The soil is of the richest red; the rainfall is plentiful; twenty years ago they decided to buy the property, build a house and make a garden.

On arrival we walked under an archway of enormous trees of every colour of grey and every variety of texture and shape. The ground was carpeted with exquisite moss. Everything was still and nurturing; an extraordinary, green tapestry-cathedral.

It gave one the kind of thrill that is experienced on going into a quiet forest. Chinese pavilions and white trellis summerhouses were hidden among towering trees and walls of pale maidenhair fern; a vine with waxen turquoise and sapphireblue blossom flourished; orchards of pale delicate grasses gave way to groves of bamboo and woodlands of trees with coloured barks. Allerton and Grieg have succeeded in making what must be the most beautiful tropical garden in the world.

FLIGHT TO TOKYO

The flight, through a night that seemed endless, and during which we lost one whole day — it seems we will get it back when we return — eventually came to an end. After flying over a boundless, periwinkle-blue sea, we saw the jagged mountains and seashores of Japan, and the sea formally patterned with rows of what turned out to be nets for oyster fishing.

The international airport was the first I had ever seen that had its own personality. There was no bustle or restlessness. The staff, all of distinguished appearance, stood quietly awaiting the arrival of the passengers. Some of the women wore rugged-looking coats over their kimonos against the cold; but to us the cold was only that of a fine crisp spring day.

I noticed a girl at a souvenir stall, at her side a few precious orchids. She looked very exotic with her face heavily coated with white paint, her cheeks made pink and her lips brilliant coral. Appearing to be startlingly inhuman, she had all the fantasy and intrinsic thrill of the stage.

The city outskirts were so vast that it took one hour to get through to the centre.

ASAKUSA

Asakusa — Japan's Piccadilly Circus or Time Square. Artificial flowers — scarlet, magenta, silver, puce — hanging in bundles outside shops; yellow and scarlet garlands of cellophane decorating restaurants; birds, butterflies, stars announcing a cabaret or newly opened business; tall bouquets on poles; lilies and chrysanthemums of the most vivid colours draw attention to new cinemas. All glitter and gloss. Despite its carnival aspect visitors to Asakusa make time to visit the Kwannon Temple to pray to the Goddess of Mercy. They throw money and pray fervently that it will come back a hundredfold.

DINNER AT A RESTAURANT

This Japanese restaurant, where the service is so discreet and the décor so restrained, is the height of refinement; a flower arrangement of three iris, a rose, a spray of freesia; soothing sounds of trickling water coming from the garden.

Shoes must come off at the door; the meal is served in a room of sliding screens on lacquer tables eight inches high; the presentation of sake wine in blue and white bottles is a ritual. The meal ends in an ante-room where the chairs are covered in immaculate, white linen loose-covers, almost starched, with dark burgundy-coloured velvet cushions on top; strawberries, three inches long, highly-glazed, of brilliant cerise, and of an unimaginable taste.

KABUKI

Kabuki is a more 'debased' form of theatrical art than the classical Noh plays or Bunraku puppets. Sentimentality is often likely to intrude on a programme of plays which the audience knows by heart.

Kabuki actors lead a life utterly dedicated to the theatre. Like monks, they hardly stir outside the walls and can be found in their dressing rooms from early morning until late evening. A performance begins at eleven in the morning and goes on until four in the afternoon.

Utaemon, the great female impersonator, was pleased tonight at my flattery. He was gracious enough to receive visitors in his dressing room, empty except for two orchids. He is much respected as a leading actor, and yet much feared for his black humours.

GEISHA HOUSE

The Geisha girl appeared, aged twenty-two. Like a little sugar mouse, she had been trained for ten years to be the perfect entertainer of men and was by now witty and pretty, exquisite, beautifully dressed, the hair lacquered like black liquorice, and with delicate soft hands that have never known work. She must be able to play the samisen and to dance.

TEA CEREMONY

Mr Sen seemed extremely worried that the edge of a lacquer table, on which a red lacquer pot was placed, was scratched. It was wiped with much vigour and anxiety. I have seldom seen anything so immaculate or pristine. Mr Sen, whose knowledge of O-cha-no-yu comes from a sixteenth-century ancestor, participated with his son in this ceremonial act, which makes of tea-drinking a spiritual experience of great aesthetic significance.

The master with the surgeon's hands started in deep silence, with lowered lids, to fold a brown linen napkin across the back of his hand. Then the implements employed in the ceremony were wiped clean. The beauty of each object was unparalleled.

Tealeaves were placed slowly in a pot, hot water poured from a kettle with a burbling, gurgling sound, gently stirred with a little broom, then violently whisked with a wooden spider.

Every gesture artfully considered. The tea is drunk in shockingly loud sips, the empty cup admired for its beauty. The ceremony took an eternity.

OBSERVATIONS

The Japanese can be cruel, that is true, and I dislike their ideas of democracy. They love their tradition, which is a feature of their ancestor-worship, so that the past and its customs may not be forgotten or broken. They like peace and quiet, yet their traffic is the noisiest in the world. They love noise too. Drivers drive on the horn although hornblowing is supposed to be prohibited.

Many of the Japanese women, unexpectedly, have ruddy, robust English country-girl complexions and frizzy, late-Victorian hair. Many of the men, too, have quite a flushed hue. The women hurry down the village street wrapped in shaggy woollens over their kimonos, their legs shabby in white, creased wool socks.

Their children are adorable, quiet and pretty and gay. They have great respect for beauty, and yet many have absolutely no aesthetic sense whatsoever. Side by side is the best in taste together with the worst.

Japanese seem never idle. Mothers hurry with their babies; old women trot, even if only across the road; but no anxiety on faces, no frown.

GION

Tokyo
The old crones look quite distinguished, with hair piled high. They sit huddled in shawls; some have fallen asleep, but that

would matter very little for business seems bad tonight, judging by the number of men's shoes exhibited in the little hallways.

A young Japanese boy reels down the street in an exaggerated display of drunkenness. He wheels to the left and, without a crash, bolts straight through the lighted door in front of him. The elderly hostess cackles with laughter as the boy falls backward on the tatami, his legs high in the air. She pulls his legs down. He lies prostrate. But the old woman tugs at his overcoat with one hand and with the other pulls back a paper door to reveal an apple-cheeked girl who will look after this poor besotted boy, and eventually extract from him the requisite fee.

THE SUMIYA

In the 'gay' quarter, where the poor man's brothels are situated, there is the old eighteenth-century whore house, the Sumiya. It is now considered a national treasure. To preserve the traditional Japan it is said to be under the care of the government.

A grandly dressed lady in scarlet and gold brocades, and wearing a towering headdress, appeared in the gloaming; her face-powder dead white, her lower lip dark red, her teeth black. She was not beautiful in the accepted sense. She was small-eyed, her face bladder-shaped, but she possessed a sense of mystery which was exciting. She never spoke but summoned her two attendants. These were little girls with black silk hair cut in fringes, and bobbed. Their faces painted chalk white; both wearing scarlet.

She walked on high wooden platforms that announced with a clack her every step. She was preceded by a man with a lamp, then flanked by her two scarlet-dressed diminutive attendants, she tottered majestically under a huge umbrella held aloft by a scantily dressed man in blue.

The prostitute now knelt. With the assistance of her acolytes she went through the serious business of the tea ceremony. Supposedly this was so that she would be put into the necessary receptive state of mind of aesthetic inspiration to enjoy our company. I believe if we had asked for it, an elaborate mock marriage could have been staged.

To Japanese eyes Europeans look extremely old. It is true that often Japanese appear ten years younger than we would guess their age to be. Their bones are prominent and the skin stretched tightly over the frame seldom sags. The old may have a web of wrinkles, but their faces rarely fall out of shape.

HONG KONG

Old women eating their bowls of rice, looking like dowager empresses, and the children like dolls. Streets of hanging dried fish, grottoes of pale silver and yellow fish. Tall balconies overhanging the crowded thoroughfares, stalls of flowers, orange-coloured chicks, and flattened ducks covered with grease. Chinese calligraphy on the pillars of arcades forming an enfilade like the wings of a theatre. Rickshaws in red lacquer, and trams of dark green enamel.

Lunch in a five-star restaurant in the Chinese quarter which is crowded out every day with thousands of people having exquisite meals.

In an old-fashioned, 1900, mahogany *chambre-particulière*, the swing-doors open and a waiter comes in with a tray of the most delectable foodstuffs imaginable. Egg roll, pork ribs, suckling pig, chicken, shrimps in pasta, vegetables in pastry. There is no subtlety of the culinary art that is not understood and appreciated.

Visit to Government House

The ADC is overdoing things. 'The dining room is to the left. Their Excellencies are entertaining a small party of six. This is the plan. You will sit on Her Excellency's right. As you go into the room you will see the table in front of you. Their Excellencies' chairs are a little higher than the others.' We proceed. 'Your Excellency, Mr Beaton,' bellowed at close quarters.

The decoration of the house is preposterous. Her Excellency has a passion for pink. One reception room might be that of a powder room in a night-club. Panelling and portraits in dining room, baby-toys on sideboard. Bad English food.

The ADC has soldier's boots. He disappears at lunch, but appears immediately afterwards so that the guests can be got rid of as soon as possible.

BANGKOK

A baffling, sprawling place without planning, it is difficult to know which is the centre of the town. The main hotels and restaurants are in a shabby little street of third-rate shops. The native quarters sprawl in endless activity. The business areas have enormous empty streets. The Government and Royal buildings are in splendid isolation.

We are told that this is the 'cool' time of the year, but imagination boggles at what life must be like here during the summer.

A few strenuous efforts to get a key turned in a lock, or a walk of a few yards, and one is bathed in sweat. It is heat of 120° in the shade.

Our spirits were raised by the utterly delightful expedition we made down the river to see the 'Floating Market'. Here people dwelling on the river-edge bring their 'shops' onto a small boat, and paddle themselves around, selling vegetables, fish, hardware, bottles of drink, and flowers.

The water gives life to this otherwise parched country, and everything grows in tropical profusion in the humid heat. The river is the life source. On its banks the denizens live in shacks of teak and matting on stilts. They use the water for everything except drinking.

THE TEMPLES

The Victorian Temple of the Dawn was our first glimpse of the architecture we expected to find in Bangkok. In the sunlight the pinnacle and minarets looked as they should — brilliant, glittering and confetti-coloured. The effect was gay and delightful. But staggering in its impact as this huge monument on the river bank is, it is naive and crude in detail and design. Like a circus temple it is made of strange fantasies — elephants, Chinese gods, and formalised flowers. Much of the decoration is cracked china. Victorian dishes have been broken to form rosettes. The dragons' tongues at the roof edges give a tremendous lightness and sweep to the whole architecture.

The mystery of the orange-draped priests was something that gave life to every temple one saw. However ugly they were, the presence of these quiet people made everything peculiar and curious.

But to me the whole palace was made particularly memorable by the presence of a number of gold women-dragon-bird figures on the terraces of one of the shrines. Leaning slightly forward, with their cocks' tails, bejewelled bodices, globe-like bosoms, neat heads with the tall, spiked head-dress of Cambodian dancers, they created an extraordinary atmosphere. Posed in the most exaggerated Diana Vreeland-like attitudes they were life-like and seemed at any minute about to strut off and perform in some ballet.

FLOUR FACTORY

We saw, suddenly, from the boat, a boy blindingly white, hanging up some washing on a line. He was from another world. We steered the boat around and landed, and I followed the white boy down a white lane where everything, the trees, the windows, and the walls, had become white from the primitive flour-factory at the farther side of the lane.

The first white boy was followed by others who came out of the door to stare. They were, with white faces and white bandages over their noses and mouths, an extraordinary sight. Silent and pondering, they smiled inhumanly.

Inside, the haze of white dust blinded one at first. Men were working barefoot among the mountains of powder. The flour was heaped on the floor and with a strange ritual was being put into carefully folded sacks. Women were sitting on sacks sewing other sacks; a naked child hanging about covered with flour. It was a ghostly, dream spectacle. I fear my camera will not be able to convey the scene, but it will always haunt me as being one of the strangest sights of this strange oriental world.

ANGKOR WAT

From the small aeroplane we caught our first glimpse of Angkor Wat. The plane circled over the jungle and suddenly an enormous Versailles-like structure shot by. It had huge grey terraces and towers among the forest green. Again we circled. Another temple sped by among palm trees and coconuts. A thrilling juxtaposition of a great past civilisation and the forces of nature.

Rickshaw tour to see the villages built on stilts. A river, in which people were quietly washing their clothes in the dusk, gives place to lights on stalls in the market square. All the children are particularly pretty, but Cambodian women are like lesbians with hair cut short, and the men, taller than Thais, are ape-like. All the population, from the age of ten it seems, favour gold teeth.

These gold teeth came into their own in the theatre when the performers, in their brightly-coloured costumes and carefully whitened faces, started to talk. Their teeth flashed like brilliant jewels.

Designs of scenery were crudely and garishly painted, with silk curtains, in holes, attached to doors. The play seemed to have a caricatured King of Thailand as the chief character.

The towers that we had seen last night silhouetted against the full moonlit sky were now touched with the early rays of sun. The green, jungle-cleared roads smelling fresh and pure after the night's cool were bordered by tall trees and flowering bushes.

We came to the lake which surrounds Angkor Wat; the pale green moss and foliage at the water's edge, with the blue of the sky reflected in the water, made a Monet-like scene. There were thousands of pink and white water-lilies.

Angkor Wat, the greatest monument left of the Khmer, was built by King Surya-Varman (1112-82) at a time when in England men were still living in a very primitive state, burning cakes in a cave and wearing fur loincloths. Of a darkish grey stone, porous like pumice, with the patina of a thousand years upon its surface, the scale is prodigious.

Splendid flights of steps lead higher and higher to the great pyramid of decorated stone, which towers over a vast sea of jungle and can be seen for miles. From photographs the great towers had seemed clumsy and formless, like mounds of worm-mould, or *marrons glacées*. But in the more brilliant sunlight they were gigantic and hugely impressive, and a fitting culmination to the great paths of serpent-lined vistas.

To see the whole magnificent construction takes a long time. Nevertheless, in two hours we climbed the highest pinnacles and took a hundred photographs of every photogenic vista, and of the extraordinary detail of the friezes; elephants, nagas, warriors; but to me the most interesting were the yard-high figures of celestial dancers (all like the Duchess of Windsor) in their posturing attitudes, wearing tall headdresses, jewellery, and elaborate, tight dresses. They were in the height of today's fashion. There is little reason to think that we have progressed much in the art of decoration and fashion since then.

HONOLULU

The wind was blowing the palm trees in violent gusts of anger. The rain lashed. The tropical island was at the height of its tourist season and in the middle of its rainy season too.

The tourists looked worse than ever in a covering of transparent mackintosh; the trash in the shops more than ever appalling.

By degrees the ubiquity of aloha and hula dancing and twanging guitars becomes so overwhelming that one is nauseated.

The Hawaiians are so pleased with themselves, their leis, their looks, for the incessant adoration of the tourists feeds their egos and they are sufficiently childlike to enjoy continual praise. But, oh, the wood-carvings, the hibiscus behind the ear, the palm frond hats, the portraits on black velvet, the crowds on the beach singing in unison, the stench of sweat and scent! There is nothing to surprise one any more.

The flight back to Honolulu was seventeen hours long. We arrived there two hours earlier than we left Japan.

Our eyes have changed. On the outward trip, accustomed to our own comforts, much that we saw seemed drab, rather squalid even. But the farther we travelled to the Orient, the more accustomed we became to the prevailing shabbiness.

The hotels in Bangkok and Angkor reached the lowest level with rusty bath-tubs, brick-coloured, cold water and an impoverished towel the size of a handkerchief. After the peeling walls, the broken-down beds and general decay, the return journey has been a great adventure in mounting luxury.

Things that had struck one as rather poor before, now seem the acme of luxury, the trip back to Honolulu like a return to the womb. The shops now seem so wonderfully elegant, whereas we were somewhat patronising about them on the journey out.

Part IV: 'Gigi', 1957

GIGI

August 1957

The sun of Beverly Hills was shining above the sentinel palms and through the Venetian blinds into my bungalow. The stillness was broken by large blue birds which darted from scarlet hibiscus to emerald blades of the banana tree and back to the feathery heads of a nameless tropical plant.

Six months previously Arthur Freed had asked me to design the musical film version of Colette's novel *Gigi*. Alan Lerner was to write the book and Fritz Loewe the music. I was well aware that it would be Colette's own world that I should have to re-create, and by degrees I began to see with her avid eyes; the colours and the atmosphere should be hers, not mine. Little girls in tartan dresses, in *broderie anglaise* with black boots and stockings, and great jewelled ladies supping at Maxim's or airing themselves in all manner of *équipages* in the Bois.

Together with Vincente Minnelli I drove to the Musée Grevin, to the Skating Rink, to the Parc Monceau and other landmarks looking for locations. 'This is where Gigi might have lived!' Minnelli mused and pointed to a tall seventeenth-century house overlooking Le Cour de Royan. An '*art moderne*' building suggested Aunt Alicia's apartment. Gaston, with his sugar-merchant parents, most likely would have inhabited the grandiose Victorian mansion that now housed the Musée Jacquemart.

Preparations were exhaustively detailed. Major additions had already been made to the cast of stars. We winnowed from a crowd of Folies Bergère girls and fashion models the beauties who were to portray *demi-mondaines*. We searched among the army of extras for the warts, wrinkles and noses that would give an authentic Sem character to the ensemble.

I returned to England with a sheaf of notes about Minnelli's requirements.

'*The Bois*: 150 people, dogs, prams, respectable family, two or three aristocratic men on horseback, two women in habits, twelve children.'

'*Maxim's*: 20 characters, caricatures, nobility, actresses, Indian, Polaire, Lady de Grey?'

'*Trouville*: Bathing machines, tennis, diabolo, alpaca swimming costume, etc.'

During May and June I was busy at work on the pinchbeck life of Paris and Trouville of half a century ago. Time was short and I dabbed paint on a hundred drawings as if I were a Japanese factory-worker. Then almost before the paint was dry I would fly off again to Paris to present the designs to producer and director before handing them on to the costumiers. Customs and Passport authorities got to know me well during those weeks.

As a result of the tests, I began to avoid certain dangerous colours. Experience showed that most bright reds became claret colour; greys inexplicably turned to Prussian blue; chartreuse yellow wound up like a Jaffa orange, and turquoise blue predominated with such force that it had to be labelled 'for external use only'.

Previous experience had shown me that designing for films is quite different from theatre work. Seldom, for instance, is a costume seen full length in the average motion picture and elaborate ornamentation on a hem is wasted effort. It is the same with the scenery. The focal point on the screen is inevitably about eye level. Yet no detail may be left to chance. The camera not only picks up shoddiness but it detects lack of sincerity or shallowness of feeling. This applies ubiquitously to the work of director, performer or designer.

By the end of July, when all had been set for an August 1st 'opening day', we discovered that in Paris the summer holiday is taken very seriously indeed. Madame Karinska had been persuaded to make more costumes than she had ever intended, but at a given moment, her hordes of Russian helpers vanished.

To add to our stress, Paris was now suffering from a fierce heatwave. The Parisiennes who were being fitted into wine-glass corsets were unable to breathe. When Madame Karinska, with artistic ardour, pulled the strings to her satisfaction, the actress would swoon. A tumbler of water and a patter of smacks on the face would not succeed in 'bringing round' the fallen lady before a heavy thud proclaimed another victim — 'Encore une autre est tombée!'

At long last, after the last detail had been worked out, the first day's shooting was scheduled.

It was a brave new world of indomitable spirit that foregathered in the Bois de Boulogne at dawn's early brightness. Producer, director, cameraman and huge technical crew, together with a vast sea of extras, had been waiting expectantly in a roped-off section of the park.

It was an historical scene. There were *calèches* of every sort, men and women on horseback, crowds of passers-by in 1900 costume. Cameras moved by on cranes, while megaphoned instructions added to the din.

By evening, the 'take' had been re-shot countless times. Carriages bowled by with clockwork precision, *grandes cocottes* looked like empresses in their elegant barouches, Chevalier continued to greet the passers-by with the same grinning spontaneity. Assistant director Bill McGary, in shirt-sleeves and turned-in toes, shouted himself hoarse. 'Send for the Stock Girls! Give us a dozen cocottes!' Grand ladies in huge hats would materialise. 'There's one cocotte missing!' 'Anybody seen a cocotte?'

Another part of the Bois was decorated with bunting and flags. A dozen carriages, entirely covered with real and artificial flowers, stood waiting for the Battle of Flowers.

It proved to be another kind of battle. A strong August wind blew hats off in every direction. Angry bunches of lilies swayed ominously, leaves fell from the trees to give warning that summer was near its end. But nature was ignored while a windblown director and crew, on high with moving camera, followed the procession of carriages.

As Queen of the Carnival, dressed in a tall muslin bonnet, a beauty sat in a lily-bedecked carriage. By way of homage, someone heaved a huge bouquet of roses into her lap.

Abruptly, ominous clouds blanketed the sky. A deluge was at hand.

The fashionable crowd made tents of newspapers and took refuge under the streaming trees. Spartan horsemen were soaked while still in the saddle. The Battle of Flowers ended in a waterspout.

Locations varied daily, but at the end of each day's shooting we would motor to St Cloud to see the rushes of the previous day's work. Far from being anxious and serious, the atmosphere in the projection room was one of jocularity. A democratic audience of technicians and performers would jeer and shout unflattering things about each other's efforts and appearances.

As part of '*la belle époque*', Maxim's was closed to the public for four days while bright lights transformed its mellow '*art moderne*' interior into a background for rich French bankers, gay ladies, zouaves, Egyptians, Ouida guardsmen over from London, and the moral refuse to be found in the best restaurants of the world. Supper-table roses wilted in the arc lights. Extras drooped or fell into sprawling attitudes of sleep during the intervals between takes. The confusion, noise and heat in this inferno continued until all participants were prostrate with exhaustion.

The heatwave that had enveloped Paris had given way to a spell of icy cold winds and the company found itself suffering from *la grippe*. A doctor went the rounds giving injections. Nevertheless on the appointed hour the miracle happened. Maxim's was once more open to the public, and the *Gigi* company was suddenly on its way to do the remaining interiors in Hollywood.

We had, while working in France during these past three months, completed nearly half of the film. But now the most important dramatic scenes were to be shot in the comparative calm of the Californian Sound Studios. A week later I found myself in Hollywood.

A bright young man named Bill Shanks was summoned and he presented himself as the Assistant Director on the picture. Bill Ryan turned out to be the General Manager, a kindly avuncular type, ready with assistance and advice. The chief property man, Harry Lazarre, was a marvel. He was indefatigable and stood at the ready with knees bent and legs apart like an expectant goalkeeper.

It was strange to come back as an employee to this city within a city, where, twenty years before, I had been a zealous sightseer. In my film-fanatic enthusiasm I had dogged the publicity staff, and a young man named Howard Strickling (now head of the department), had arranged interviews and photographic sittings with some of my favourite stars. When he took me to the studio cafeteria for a club sandwich and ice-cream in the company of medieval peasants, cowboys, ladies in white wigs and crinolines, German spies and the entire Barrymore family, I felt I was really seeing life from the inside. Little did I expect that one fine day, as set and costume designer for the musical version of *Gigi*, I would eat my Elizabeth Taylor salad or Cyd Charisse sandwich here each noon for weeks on end as a matter of course.

Perhaps now the greatest impression, as a newcomer, was of the distances to be covered during the course of an average day's work. Women's Character Wardrobe and Men's Wardrobe were long distances apart, though Wigs and Makeup were conveniently situated in the same building. The sound stages were often half a mile from the Art Department or the 'Still' Camera Depot and Publicity, while the outdoor locations on Lot 2 were impossible to reach on foot. Even the warehouses, where furniture of all periods, china, glass and every sort of 'property' are stored, were like vast hangars, and a man who wore a pedometer on his ankle discovered he had walked ten miles in a morning. Few people realise the value of the contents of these warehouses. I discovered a Golgotha hoard of riches dating back to the great days of extravagance. Here was Sèvres porcelain and real Louis XV furniture that had been brought back from Europe by special envoys scouting for Norma Shearer's *Marie Antoinette*.

There were specialists in charge of jewellery and of buying materials and there were those who knew precisely how dirty to make a certain costume. The 'property men', too, responsible for everything the players may use in the course of a day's acting, have developed their craft so that they have come to be relied upon as magicians.

Once I mistook a turning and found myself on the Pacific Ocean front at Santa Monica, twenty miles off course. Nevertheless at the end of the day's work I enjoyed driving, with the radio at full blast on the dashboard, towards Beverly Hills, purple in the fading light.

The weeks rushed by in a surge of overwork. Necessarily one got to know the star performers extremely well.

Leslie Caron never allowed herself to be hurried or cajoled into making a decision she had not long thought out for herself. Typical of the new Hollywood leading lady, she despised flamboyant behaviour or 'glamorous' off-screen appearances and reserved her temperament for her performance.

Isabel Jeans was always good-tempered, however arduous or disappointing her days might be. Often ready 'made up' after a dawn call, she would wait upon bad weather or a delayed schedule until dusk without appearing before the cameras. But then when the time came she gave as spontaneous and distinguished a performance as if it had been rehearsed for months before.

Maurice Chevalier, the complete professional, was never out-of-sorts or inconsiderate, and had a broad smile for all.

I never enjoyed for long the quietness of my sumptuous office. 'We've a problem here. Can you come down?' Even my lunches in the commissary were interrupted with the intercom messages — 'Seesil Bayton wanted on telafon' and the messages would often come as a surprise — 'Please will you be outside stage 15 at 1.20 to inspect a tennis court?' 'Will you okay a sugar bracelet to be eaten by a Lippit-zane horse?' I discovered I could cut a stuffed peacock in half, and still make it stand up on a *demi-mondaine's* head and I found that I could trim thirty hats in one and a half hours.

By now we had shot the Trouville scenes on the Pacific shore and they had appeared successfully like paintings of Boudin.

We remained often two or three days shooting on each set. The effect was as if we had been staying in the houses of the various characters. From the bourgeois parlour of crimson and plush of Gigi's grandmother we moved to the Fragonard elegance of Aunt Alicia's apartment for lessons in jewellery, deportment, and the choosing of wine and clothes; then to Uncle Honoré's where the decoration was '*art moderne* 1900' with mustard and Chartreuse colour schemes.

The leading actors had had time to become the characters they were impersonating. It is the final lap of filming that creates the most danger points. Energy begins to sag, impatience sets in, even if imperceptibly, and actors and actresses, even without their knowing it, are apt to cheat on their performances, to play for sympathy, to sweeten their characterisation and beautify their appearances.

Vincente Minnelli's vitality brooked all setbacks, even re-takes. With the aid of countless Dixie-cups of black coffee, his enthusiasm and meticulous attention to detail was unabated. 'Do you consider the relationship of those characters in that sequence is real?' he would ask in a hushed whisper. He was alive to every nuance of acting behaviour, to every infinitesimal visual aspect and every technicality.

'We're going to shoot the Pre Catalan and the Bal Masque on Friday,' Bill Ryan told me. 'It'll be a busy day for you — but after that there'll only be the intimate scenes to do.'

When Friday arrived I realised that Bill Ryan had been speaking in euphemisms. Two hundred extras had to be dressed and on the lot in time for Vincente to shoot the elaborate sequence of the masked ball. This comic motley crowd of 1900-looking Pierettes, Cromwellian Cavaliers, Nell Gwynns and Marie Antoinettes throwing confetti and streamers, had to surge up and down a giant staircase with a precision that must always look spontaneous. The shot must be completed before the midday break, after which all had to be changed again for a completely different but equally difficult one that afternoon.

One is only vaguely conscious that the producer has set a certain time in which the picture should be made, but few connected with its execution ever really believe in the schedule. 'It will take months longer,' says everyone from the sound-track expert to the continuity girl. Just as the schoolboy at his first boarding-school can never believe in the end of term, or the prisoner that the day of his release will ever arrive, so, too, those involved cannot envisage the possible completion of a picture.

The film had yet to be edited and polished, songs and incidental music had to be synchronised. It is a movieland truism that the talent of those responsible for 'shaping' a film creates much of its success.

The experiences of the last six months had been interesting and happy. New vistas had been opened and perhaps now that my work was abruptly over, ordinary everyday existence would seem, by comparison, just a bit humdrum.

Part V: Old Friends: New Places, 1958-60

PAROS WITH TRUMAN CAPOTE

Paros, Greece: August 26th, 1958

We have not seen a newspaper since we arrived on this island a week ago. We have lived in a timeless haze of repetition. Life is nothing but sleep, swim, eat and read. The meals take little time to eat for they are not interesting, and we are in a hurry, after lunch, to get to our bedrooms. We meet again five or six hours later; time passes very quickly with slumber and books. One day merges soothingly into another without incident. Each day is a pattern.

This morning I was on my roof terrace painting the white marshmallow village below. Only a few people were awake. As on every other day, the first to appear was an old man with huge stomach and straw hat; he sits like a statue, blinking at the horizon; an elderly Greek couple come out from between their blue shutters to spend the whole day on their balcony; and the local photographer and his wife busy themselves watering from tins their carefully tended zinnias.

Today Truman talked about writing. 'The mood is something that must be created by technique. To bring *Christmas Story* alive, I wrote it in the present tense. I felt so strongly about it, because the loss of this woman, when I heard of it at school, was one of the most dreadful things that have ever happened to me in my life. When I was writing the last page of that story, with the kites flying up to heaven, I was so upset that I vomited and cried for three days. It is only now that I have read and re-read so many hundreds of times what I have written that I can see the technique and prevent myself from weeping. I am convinced there is no one in America who knows so much about the style and the technique of writing as I do, or who writes as well.'

Truman considers that E.M. Forster is about the best writer today; his ear is sharp, each sentence is perfectly formed, his characters are real and the situations valid. But he thinks no one since Shakespeare had a better ear than Virginia Woolf — every line she wrote was immaculate, even if the content was not extraordinary. Maugham, without a true ear, had taught himself how to write well. Though his ear was good and he knew how to write polished prose, David Cecil's writing is lifeless — a pastiche — nothing to do with the idiom of today.

Truman had written *Breakfast at Tiffany's* as an exercise, and only the dialogue was in the style of today. J.D. Salinger was the great exponent of the modern vernacular. The greatest genius of all, who really knew how to write, and who had complete insight into the characters of all his creations, was Proust, the undoubted master.

We talked about the inner rhythm in Shakespeare. Truman said that it was this inner rhythm that was an essential part of good writing. 'My ear is so strong that it is apt to run away with me, to make me depend too much on what it tells me rather than on "style". A statement has to give information in the most lucid terms. But it can do so in so many rhythms. The choice of word combinations is limitless; that is why it is hard to choose and make a final decision. That is why I write so slowly. With all these words flying around that is what writing is about. That is why I give so much time to it and take it so seriously; it is the one thing I can't have a sense of humour about. That article on Brooklyn I showed you took me a month; but then I never rewrite; no time is spent crossing out and rewriting or polishing.'

Truman has a good idea of what an artist he is; he could make a great deal of money if he needed to; but money doesn't mean much to him at the moment; he turns down lucrative offers and only does what interests him. He is not hard up and lives extravagantly for much of the year.

The people of Paros have come out to enjoy the cool and magic of dusk. They sit along the esplanade drinking ouzo. They pay little attention to us. They are inquisitive only to a point, then are completely unfriendly. Truman and Jack usually make friends easily with the inhabitants of every place they visit, but here they know no one outside the personnel of this hotel. The locals are too removed from the world to care. They are physically unattractive.

The little town has immense charm and even mystery; it is a labyrinth of white-washed dwellings; white walls, white doors and even white paving-stones. The only contrast is provided by the dark greens of cypresses, honeysuckle, or morning glory over a balcony. The church, built at the time of Santa Sophia, has a touch of modernity and the pie-crusted arches of the cloisters might have been designed by Emilio Terry. Inside there are tall pews with inexplicable high rests for the arms — can it mean one sits with hands at eye level?

We drove down a mountainside through olive groves and suddenly found ourselves in a green oasis where trees grew to gigantic heights — ilex, cypress, olives. There were pomegranates, quince, figs, and there was water rushing through great fertility of green shade. We noticed what looked like strange pear-shaped black and white leaves on a wall; these 'leaves' gradually opened and we saw that they were bright coral pink, orange and scarlet butterflies. The driver shook the foliage and suddenly the air was a-flutter with scarlet wings. The butterflies, which had become the shape of the leaf on which they slept, flew out in their hundreds and thousands. It was a strangely beautiful sight, and perhaps unique to this one place. It was so cool and green and romantic here that we hated to leave. It was a rare experience.

ROSE MACAULAY

October

Rose Macaulay, string and bones for years, had become almost like a galvanised corpse. Someone said of her, as she came into a crowded party at Ann Fleming's, 'Heavens, there's the ghost of E.F. Benson as Hamlet!'

Rose Macaulay's interest and enthusiasm for life alone made up the driving power that kept her going, for she never seemed to touch food or drink. She was never warmly enough clad in winter, and always cold in the height of a Greek summer. At last the impetus had come to an abrupt stop. But Dame Rose dines and lunches out all week as usual, driving her battered car everywhere. She would wait in it if she had arrived early, and in a leisurely way bring out a lipstick and 'freshen-up' her face.

On Tuesday, Simon Fleet and Juliet Duff gave a cruise reunion party. All their friends who had been to Greece and Russia together were gathered in the Gothic Box. The party was not a disappointment — in fact a surprising success. But on Thursday morning, Dame Rose was dead. Her photograph, shot onto the television screen, gave me a shock.

GRETA BY HERSELF

New York: Winter, 1958-9

Greta has gone from one doctor to another. Suddenly she started to feel better when she was given insulin injections by a quack. 'I can't come to you every day to take my turn in the queue,' she said. 'I have [*with a laugh*] too much to do!' (She has nothing whatsoever to do!) The doctor said: 'You come in by the side door here, and I'll always fit you in. Don't miss a day though, not even Sundays.'

So on Sunday Greta went and found the doctor in his dressing gown. 'Excuse me being undressed and unshaved like this. It's wonderful not to have to shave, and to be dirty for one day in the week.' Greta sympathised, got her shot, and left.

Next day, on arrival, she told the liftman she wanted to see the doctor. 'The doctor ain't no more. He died last night.' Greta felt faint. She was stunned for several days afterwards, and felt absolutely lost.

She did not know which way to turn. She suddenly resumed her relationship with her friend Mercedes. For a year or more she had cut her. If she met Mercedes while walking with Eric Goldsmith, she would nod only in the most cursory manner. Then, suddenly, Greta telephones, comes round to Mercedes, bursts into floods of tears.

'I have no one to look after me.'

'You don't *want* anyone to look after you.'

'I'm frightened! I'm so lost!'

Mercedes is her very best friend, and for thirty years has stood by her, willing to devote her life to her.

Once again Greta rallied. Mercedes prevailed upon a little doctor to break his rule of not having private clients and to come to New York from Rochester each day to look after Greta.

'How do I know what you're doing to me? How do I know you're not killing me?'

The little man, very Italian and gallant, kissed her on the cheek and said: 'I think you're the sweetest person I ever knew.' But when he asked for her telephone number, she refused to give it. 'Very well then, I shall not continue to look after you. I've never heard such nonsense in my life. If your doctor can't telephone to know how you are responding to his treatment, there's no point in his continuing.'

'Very well, but you're not to give that number to Mercedes.'

'Do you mean to say you haven't given your number to the person who begged me to look after you?'

'I'll give it to her later.'

The doctor rang Mercedes. 'Would you mind if I ask you a very personal question? Have you, or not, Miss Garbo's telephone number?'

'No!'

'I'm shocked! That is the most selfish thing I've heard in my life. It's absolutely inhuman!'

In spite of everything, Mercedes continues to do all she can for Greta. Greta arrived unexpectedly at her flat, very upset. She had been to the Health Food store and the woman there had said: 'Oh, Miss Garbo, you don't look at all well!' Greta was in tears. 'Do I look so changed? Do I look so old?' Mercedes secretly ran to the Health Food store and, shaking a finger, instructed the woman. 'Don't you ever tell Miss Garbo she doesn't look well again! However badly you think she looks, tell her she looks fine.' The woman was dreadfully apologetic and upset.

Mercedes suffers dreadfully at Greta's cruelty, and after all these years has not adopted an invulnerable attitude. Yet she can be funny about Greta's extraordinary behaviour and instead of getting angry (as I am apt to do), she giggles. 'Well, we really must admit she's a character, if not a real eccentric.'

The saddest aspect of this escape from people is in the fact that by now very few people are left who care about her whereabouts. A few old cronies still discuss her at length, but a whole generation has now grown up who have never seen her. When she walks down the street today, very few people recognise her.

Her health precludes her from leading a 'normal' life, her habit of being by herself has become so much more exaggerated and she has eaten an artichoke for dinner at 7.15 almost every night alone in her own apartment. She has not been to a theatre for a year, and done very little shopping.

November

On arrival in New York I telephoned. Greta seemed delighted that her silence had been broken in upon. She came around that afternoon and stood at my doorway looking like a terrified creature: her eyes wide open and mouth agape as if ready for any torture. We laughed; we drank a little vodka, although she should abstain, and she would have stayed for dinner if I had not already made another engagement.

I felt a great tenderness for her most of the time and very little exasperation. My heart was touched by her. I enjoyed telephoning to her many times a day to find out how she fared, to keep in touch, to 'clock in', even if I knew there was nothing much to say.

For a month I telephoned most days. Sometimes she would suggest a meeting — a dinner with some Swedish friends.

I knew that at the present moment it was unwise to try and discuss our situation. I was in danger of taking on what would probably be an appallingly difficult life task. But no decision would be possible now. She was too ill and disorganised, too abject, too much embedded in her frigid rut to lose her head enough to make any affirmative gesture.

It is not the time for anything but treading water, and for enjoying minor pleasures.

Later Greta went off to the South of France to join 'her friend'. They joined Aristotle Onassis on his yacht and had a gayer time than for many a year.

When September passed into November there had been no word from Greta, who returned to New York and, for want of anything better to do, retired to her bed.

Greta is more and more difficult to cope with. One admires the strength of her opinions. During the lifetime she spent in Hollywood, she did not let the attitude of the place nor the vulgarity of the people impinge upon her in any way. She remained completely pure. But at what a price! As she has said, it has created a sort of living death for her. Having for so many years built up strong barriers of resistance, she is now unjust to the overtures of other people. It is impossible to sway her point of view, to make her change her mind. She cannot be coerced. Thus she is a difficult companion, becoming more so as the years go by.

GRETA TO MEET VICTOR

January 31st, 1959
Greta had decided to wash her hair in honour of the outing arranged to meet Victor Rothschild. The electricity in the air

made the hair stand on end. She wore a turquoise blue handkerchief round her neck. She looked like a young Trilby.

Victor and his wife came in, delighted to see me after a long interval. They then discovered the presence of Greta. Huge delight and surprise. Victor, coarse as he is, spoke in a robust, somewhat challenging vein. 'Why did you go on Onassis' yacht? What do you get out of it?' Greta was a little nonplussed. She is generally witty and quick of answer, but the bull-like Victor was too strong a breath of air for her.

Victor addressed himself to me. He joked and laughed. We had a good time, conversation being more or less general. Then Greta got up and left. No regrets from the Rothschilds at her departure, but on to more jolly jokes. Immediately after the Rothschilds had left, Greta telephoned. 'Don't let them know who you're speaking to, if they're still there.' 'But what happened?' 'I didn't enjoy myself. The "Lord" never even looked at me. He paid no attention to me whatsoever. It wasn't at all a nice atmosphere. I was numb, and I've come home very depressed.' It made me very sad that she was sad. I apologised. 'Well, when you're as sensitive as I am it isn't very pleasant, especially when you go out as little as I do. You expect it to be an exception and very gay.' Then I said: 'Well, please forget it, and I'm sorry,' and she said: 'Give me another chance. Goodnight, Beattie.' My heart broke.

SOUTH OF FRANCE

Mummie almost died at Monte Carlo during the night. Sudden sickness that lasted two hours reduced her to a shadow. The doctor had remained until 2.30 am. Nancy was very upset. When I arrived, Mummie looked almost lifeless, but revived wonderfully during the next ten minutes and after a cup of tea.

By the end of the day she was improved, and on the road to recovery. But Nancy had been alarmed when she vomited blood and Mummie had said: 'I'm so ill, don't leave me.'

I was terribly haunted by the Hotel Metropole life. These old people are fighting to live in decent circumstances; not richness, but a respectable gentility and a certain aristocratic formality.

JOHN GIELGUD

New York: May 1959

I have often seen John Gielgud in Shakespeare and have been impressed. He has sometimes been encumbered by bad costumes; occasionally his mannerisms have irritated me, and moments of great feeling have passed while I was exhausted or paying no heed. This performance, however, of readings from Dadie Rylands' *Ages of Man*, was for me different and superb. So great was the effect of his words upon me that I was totally transported from the world of my own activities, my own thoughts and interests.

This was great acting, in the tradition of the Bettertons and Irving, but in contemporary taste. There was the minimum of ranting and of haminess. The lightness of the faery poetry, the drama of Cassius' speech, the speeches on the kingship of Richard II and Henry IV, and the dignity of Othello were magnificently conveyed. There was something touching about the king wishing, as he sat near the field of battle, that he could enjoy the life of the country rustic.

By the time Gielgud came to Lear's speech on old age — 'Howl, Howl, Howl!' — I, together with the whole audience, had become his slave. It was one of the greatest joys I have ever had in the theatre.

BARONESS BLIXEN

New York

Karen (Baroness Blixen) came to lunch with me today. She brought a young cousin with her. She allowed me to take lots of photographs.

The baroness appeared smiling and appealing with a pink and white complexion and huge blackened eyes. She was like a medieval spider, all in black. She wore a most wonderful black felt pirate's hat that came down onto her eyes. She is thinner than ever before and her legs, in black stockings, were mere sticks of liquorice. She now cannot eat. She subsisted on oysters and champagne for the first weeks here, but now she cannot stomach the idea of another oyster. Today she drank a little consommé and ate a few grapes, but her diet is not enough for her to keep alive on. Karen said when she goes back to Denmark, she will go straight to bed and remain there until her death. The nice, healthy cousin blows a 'pouff' into the air. 'Nonsense, nonsense!'

'Oh it doesn't matter,' said the baroness. 'I'm so enjoying being here, getting such a feeling of life that I'm storing up impressions that will last me for the rest of my life.'

Karen blinked and looked around the room like an unseeing bird, her eyes full of thoughts far away. It is perhaps this that gives a romantic look to the eyes, and takes away the feeling of actuality.

Karen is such a rare and wonderful emanation of her own imagination that she has come to look just like one of the characters from her writing. For me there is nothing more elegant. She is the best-dressed woman (she has a pet dress designer in Copenhagen). She is the last of the great romantics. I feel sad to think that the number of times I will see her again is very limited indeed. Karen admits that her body is kept going just with her enjoyment of life and exhilaration and determination to survive.

GRETA

I called up a few days after arrival — great surprise. Joy! She was doing nothing. But she had a cold — the same sad impasse. She would come round for a glass of vodka. The door bell rang. Waldemar Hansen answered it. She stood there transfixed, with her mouth wide open, a look of mock terror in her eyes — no move — no word. I stood motionless copying her mood, my mouth wide open too. 'Well, well!' said Waldemar and left. We sat on a sofa indulging in badinage.

'You look very pretty,' she said.

'Oh no, I'm a wreck. I can't *stand* my appearance.' Nothing of any interest was said. No direct questions asked by me; a certain amount of narrative about the holidays; how she wore a Pucci dress once when they were invited to lunch with Winston Churchill. But no one had anything to say. He was sleepy and old. He remembered her from the films. The secretary apologised for asking them at the last minute, but they never knew what sort of a mood Churchill would be in.

Greta's face was flawless. It is still a beautiful, secretive face and the play of expression that runs over it while she tells a story is an enchantment to watch. The lips move over the teeth with perfect delicacy of meaning.

The telephone calls have continued as frequently as ever. But they are kindness, or perhaps habit.

'How are you feeling — less tired?'

'I won't tell you.' But by degrees I learn.

'I'm having my quota of alcohol, then I'm going to beddy-byes. You're going out? Don't tell me all these things or I'll be right over and join you.'

MUMMIE AT REDDISH

July 1959

It is a tragedy to watch people getting too old to be master of themselves. My mother, until she was eighty, was a phenomenon. She looked and acted like a woman of sixty. She had great vitality. She ran the house and looked after the garden. She was a character to contend with. She did her embroidery, making with astonishing speed her rugs and carpets. We could not supply her fast enough with library books.

But Mummie has no friends and was always lazy about keeping in touch with the family. Then, unfortunately, she came to London one winter, the day before one of the worst fogs there has ever been. Many of the prize cattle being shown at the Smithfield Fair were killed by being unable to breathe; thousands of older people were taken ill during the night to hospital. My mother was put in an oxygen tent. Then by ambulance she returned to the country.

From that experience, her heart has never recovered. Twice she caught pneumonia and was on the point of death; once I flew back from New York at a moment's notice expecting the worst. But her constitution is remarkable. Her will to live saw her through to recovery.

But lately she seems to be quietly deteriorating. Each time I go away I return to find her looking iller, older. By degrees she is capable of less and less effort. She is tired out, yet is restless.

Her heart condition makes her want to be on the move, from one room to another.

MY PLAY

September

I started to design a new set and costumes for my play about Gainsborough without really knowing if the production was going ahead. The cast, by painful degrees, was assembled under the calm and professional guidance of Douglas Seale as director. Nothing really seemed tangible and, with the exception of the session of recording the music when Sauget came over from Paris, none of the activities was really agreeable.

Then suddenly things started to go wrong with my play. Wolfit had, during the third week of rehearsals, turned against it and was doing his best to undermine the enthusiasm of the cast. He threatened to walk out of it at a moment's notice. He let it be known that he had no contract. Jack Minster, busy with a difficult production of a bad Bates' play, is, at best, a poor fighter. He allowed himself and all of us to be blackmailed by the bully Wolfit.

When on tour, after three performances, Wolfit took it into his head to ring up the Press and say he was unhappy with the play, we might as well have known the whole project had been scuttled. But the pain was protracted. Rays of hope would break through the storm clouds; names of possible actors would be bandied as replacements; London theatres suggested. When the notices in the Dublin morning papers were bad (after a good opening reception), I was resigned that the whole thing was over. But no, I must suffer another interminable ten days.

I returned home at seven o'clock after an afternoon of appointments to find Peter Hall telephoning from Stratford, and Hal Prince giving idiotical dates for his production of *Tenderloin*; the Comédie Française rang me about *School for Scandal*, and I arranged there and then to execute these designs at Christmas-time. Thus, within ten minutes, my winter was arranged, but only at the thirteenth hour did I receive news of my play.

GRETA: DINNER WITH THE LASZLOS

New York

The same false promises. Let's go to Switzerland. Let's go to the automat (for the best coffee in New York). Let's go tomorrow. But after all these years I know she will never go. Moreover the bonhomie induced by drink will have departed in the morning.

The ragging went on all evening. It would have been easy to speak the truth, but in front of the Laszlos impossible.

The latter part of the evening was made amusing by Greta telling old stories of how she could not sleep for the country noises when staying with Cecile de Rothschild. I had forgotten the incidents, but her memory is fantastic. (She still talks to Mercedes about some lamb chops we had when the three of us dined at the Colony.) She was able to recapture exactly the sounds of the various clocks; the one on her chimney-piece that buzzed and whirred before striking every quarter-of-an-hour, and the church clock which tolled the hours and half-hours until suddenly she imitated the first rooster which presaged the dawn chorus. Never have I heard a rooster's cry copied so exactly, so funnily. Once again I felt so sad that because of her neuroses this great actress had for fifteen years given up her *raison d'être* — her acting.

'Why did I go out last night? What for?' 'But you enjoyed it. You led them on. You even told them you were going to Switzerland with them.' I felt a bit bearish; I wouldn't play the game. Greta worried, couldn't quite finish her sentences. 'Has he become a snob?' At one moment she got up from the sofa to have a reassuring look at herself. No she had not lost her beauty.

RHINEBECK

New York: October 19th, 1959

I am glad to be here and grateful to Helen Hull for her kindness, her musical interests, her lacquer, and pretty garden flowers in Chinese bowls. It is a complete contrast to the New York hotel and I am beginning to thaw.

Many memories of the past are brought alive by this visit. I used to come to nearby Rhinebeck so often, as a friend of Alice Astor Obolensky. Now Alice is dead and so too are many of the people that used to stay with her there. I remember when Pavlik and I were reconciled to one another after some ridiculous, long-drawn-out feud, as a result of listening to a Tchaikovsky gramophone record; and Doris Castlerosse is a faint memory. Now Ivan Obolensky is in charge of that house and Brook Astor is unaccountably a rich widow at the late Vincent Astor's house. The changes are tremendous. Yet the Hudson river still binds me with its allure, its charm. It is the part of the countryside that I like best. Now I am seeing it for the first time with the leaves on the trees. Generally I associate Rhinebeck with snow, ice and the coldest winds I have ever known.

SUCCESSES AND FAILURES

January 12th, 1960

The late fifties were fortunate years for me. I was riding on the crest of a high wave. Although working hard, even to the point of exhaustion, things seemed to go easily and I was pleased with my output and its quality. I suffered from strain and pressure but was never positively ill.

With the success of *My Fair Lady* and *Gigi*, my self-confidence enabled me to ignore small setbacks. However, at the end of last year, disappointments and reverses began to rain down on me.

The biggest disappointment was the failure of my Gainsborough play. Reeling with the shock of complete failure, frustrated, and in an excess of fatigue, I flew to New York where it was fortunate that I could straight away be embroiled with the visual side of the musical based on Edna Ferber's *Saratoga*. New York, visited by me for the fourth time in one year, was hot beyond bearing, empty of friends.

Everyone working on *Saratoga* was confident this would be the biggest success since *The Music Man*. In spite of it being the brainchild of the same director, this was not to be. *Saratoga*, after five successful weeks in Philadelphia, was roasted by the New York critics. No success to chalk up here.

I returned to London to start immediately on Peter Hall's production for Stratford of *The Two Gentlemen of Verona*. One afternoon, when working with Alan Tagg on the models, I went up to my bedroom to sleep for ten minutes. I slept till next morning. When the scheme Alan and I had completed was at first admired, then rejected, I went for a week's rest and starvation at Enton Hall to give me the enthusiasm for a second attempt at discovering what was at the back of the very young and very busy director's mind. Alan proved a resourceful and undaunted assistant. After another complete overhauling of ideas, the models were accepted.

A week later a letter from the director: 'I have bad news.' The fire curtain must be able to be lowered at any given moment during the evening. By the very nature of the production suggested by Peter Hall, this was impossible. Rather than 'rethink' the entire production once again, and in spite of the fact that I had completed the designs for thirty out of the forty costumes, I had to admit that unless they could come to some Fire Law solution with my existing plans, I would have to resign as I had no inspiration left to continue. Five weeks of work were completely wasted; but with the news that the musical *Tenderloin* for New York and the Comédie Française *School for Scandal*, for which I was to do sets and costumes, were both being postponed there was suddenly the chance to take a holiday.

BALENCIAGA

Paris: February

Often I am foolish enough to arrive in Paris without warning anyone of my visit, and sometimes for the first day or two I do not seem able to forge into the life of the city. (I dislike having a meal by myself in a restaurant and I am certainly not adventurous in touring the night spots alone.) However, on this occasion I had warned dear old Marie Louise Bousquet beforehand of my impending appearance. Awaiting me at the hotel was the typically generous note from this most loving of all friends, saying: 'I am free — free — free. I await you at your convenience — at drink time — or for any dinner — all my lunches are free — free — free.' Before I had time to unpack the telephone rang. It was Marie Louise saying that Cristobal Balenciaga would like us to dine.

Cristobal is a quiet, calm, even serene person; as soon as one arrives in his apartment one comes under his spell. There is no greater pleasure than being in his company.

When we arrived, he was sitting in front of the fire, dressed all in black as is his wont, absorbed in the details of Camus's 'unnecessary' death in the evening paper. Obviously it gave him quite a shock to be brought back to the present, but by degrees he surfaced enough to tell us that Ramon would be with us soon. He fixed the dry martinis and we talked generalities.

His flat, decorated in dark greens and pale greys, was furnished in a bold style typical of him: heavy candlesticks, solid fire-irons, a huge lump of crystal on the low table, the very chaste *appliqués*, the two large bushes of azaleas, one white, one pink, in porphyry pots. It is a phenomenon that the son of an ordinary Spanish boatman, a poor boy with no opportunity to glimpse the grand world, should be born with such innate taste. Now his clothes influence the entire world of fashion, and he has a highly refined sense in all forms of art. This apartment was proof of his purity of vision. He admitted how much he enjoyed going out to antique shops and discovering finds: yet his rooms are so sparse and uncluttered that you know that everything has been chosen as the result of ruthless elimination and complete discrimination.

Marie Louise, by way of conversation, informed Cristobal that I had recently decorated a show in New York with over one hundred and fifty costumes. Cristobal winced, shut up his face like a sea anemone, and said: 'What a terrible work! How *tired* you must be! That must be such a tremendous nervous strain: it must take so much out of you!' In fact it doesn't take all that much out of me; I happen to be overtired at this point for the foolish reason that I had undertaken to do too much for too long. I am aware, too, of the enormous amount of vital energy it takes for Cristobal to create his clothes: that is why they are so good: they are the result of depth of thought, intense concentration, even physical suffering.

Marie Louise observed that I was now going to lead a clinic existence in Switzerland. Cristobal perked up to his favourite subject: it appears his hobby is the snow. He talked about the calming influence of mountains in snow, the effect of the quietness on the nerves. Cristobal said that it was necessary for him to spend at least one long holiday, if not two, in the winter, calming down in the mountains. He described the pleasure of sitting in bed with the window open to the cold or to the sun, and the luxury that was provided in these dazzling heights: hothouse flowers and fruit, cherry jam and croissants, and caviar with hot potatoes. His enthusiasm corroborated the fact that it was the right thing for me to do at this juncture when my health is none too good and my nervous system in need of padding.

Cristobal's friend, the young Ramon, came into the room, smiling and swarthy. Marie Louise began to tease him. He looked somewhat embarrassed. Cristobal smiled his crinkled surgeon's smile. Marie Louise's ribaldries are refreshing to this solemn, monk-like Spaniard. No one else behaves in her outrageous manner in this reserved, quiet apartment.

Marie Louise gave a virtuoso's performance: she became a witch throwing her head back in hollow, hoarse laughter. She bubbled with pure fun and French wit.

One always has the feeling of privilege when one is with a person who sees few people. One feels proud at being the exception to the rule. Tonight I realised that although Cristobal refuses to see anything of the *monde* and never faces his clients, he knows all the latest *potins* and scandals almost before anyone else.

An exception to his rule was when he made a dress for someone to wear at a gala. He told us of it: 'It had huge panels hanging loosely back and front, and a tight tube underneath.' (He goes through the motions of a snakecharmer.) Two days before the gala, he went to the fitting room to see the lady, who turned triumphantly to him: 'Don't you think it's beautiful what I've done to the dress?' The panels had been sewn together and shaped to follow the line of her waist, and they had been covered with expensive embroidery. 'Don't you think it's beautiful?' Cristobal leapt at the dress, tore it to shreds, and said to the *vendeuse* (who was a particular friend of his): 'And you will pay out of your own pocket for all that embroidery!'

Cristobal talked a great deal about Chanel, whom he sees occasionally, and for whom he has a great admiration. He described the dresses that she was making when he first came onto the dressmaking scene and which gave him such stimulus. With his wiry, iron fingers, he could merely by his gestures turn a piece of material in circles. He can conjure up vividly an effect, an epoch. He went through the pantomime of Chanel today (seventy-five years old) still making the same clothes but working, working so hard over the armholes, and wondering where to put a certain button, where to end a cuff. He was able to evoke in a vivid way this great character, this indefatigable publicity hound who he said would 'die' if she did not see her name in print every day. He applauded her courageous independence, immaculate cleanliness and appetising physical allure. He marvelled at her understanding of art, be it Greek or Egyptian or Chinese, be it lacquer, quartz, gold or precious stones.

It is said that Cristobal has recently had the Bogolometz treatment; certainly he seems vastly improved and in good spirits. But as we left after a long evening of anecdotes and laughter, Marie Louise said: 'But you know, to find him like that is very rare. He doesn't often come out of his shell, and at a time when he is right in the middle of making his collections. That was very extraordinary.'

ST MORITZ

February

Strangely enough, in this clean mountain air one has little appetite and all food seems so savourless. One is out of breath in the high altitude. The severe cold outside, and the merciful heating inside, do not help my hacking cough and phlegm retching. People at home envy me this most expensive holiday; they long to get away and I feel a pig that I don't enjoy it more. But let us make an effort and remember the delights, for there have been several.

It was the greatest joy to wake up in the train, having left Paris the night before, to go into the restaurant car for breakfast and gaze at the snow-spattered mountain villages. They seemed to be comprised of toy wooden houses, brick churches with very tall spires, clean gardens and clean washing hanging out in the cold air. On seeing the children muffled up in scarlet, bouncing along the steep inclines, one thought of Bruegel. The waiters in the train were young and healthy boys. They served with almost acrobatic sleight of hand the generous dollops of sizzling hot coffee and milk. Nothing in the world tasted better than the rolls, butter and dark cherry jam. As the train sped higher it became almost a funicular in the snowy glades: the white cushion-laden trees were illustrations to

Grimm's tales. One had suddenly heightened curiosity about one's fellow human beings — they appeared strange and unexpected.

I had not been to a winter sports world for twenty years, and it struck me anew how remarkable it is that people can speed over the crisp, powdery crust under their own steam with nothing but two blades of wood under them.

There was something dreamily reminiscent about the hotel when I arrived. I had, in fact, been here before, but my memory of it was faint. I liked its Scottish Gothic turrets, fretsaw filigree. Icicles fell from the deep, wooden eaves; big, black crows flapped on the balcony and rather guardedly came for the scattered remains of my breakfast croissants. The lack of sound, the complete quietness, was balm to the soul: there is no silence like that created by snow. All is quiet except for the crunch of one's own boots and the tinkle of an approaching sleigh. This is a pretty sight, white horses with plumed head-dresses, the driver wearing an almost ridiculously romantic, hussar-like bearskin, and a black cape of long-haired fur.

At night the moon cast a blue veil over the whole snow-blanketed, lamp-lit picture. A distant dance band could be heard, but muffled, and the solitary barking dog did not break the spell.

I enjoyed the improbable progress of the funicular railway. I enjoyed seeing, too, the eccentric English abroad. It was they who invented winter-sports, and they are still the first to rush down a mountain on their stomachs with their noses one inch from a wall of ice. I enjoyed the taste of the sizzling cream and cheese-covered eggs eaten out-of-doors at the Coneglia Club.

It was interesting to see how the richest people in the world have the desire to get back to nature, and spend part of the year on these mountain slopes. Leaving behind their fabulously extravagant drawing rooms in Paris, New York and London, they seem perfectly happy in a reasonably primitive chalet. Tanker multi-millionaires converse with steel or motor millionaires.

My invalid spell ended. I began to feel healthy again. Suddenly the place died on me, and I left with no regret.

MY MOTHER IN HER 87TH YEAR

The creakings of the floorboard on the landing have become a new, but important element in the life of the house. It is something that I will always remember with a certain dread and sadness. Quite recently my mother has become even more restless, and one of its forms is that she will not remain in her bed for more than a few minutes. Exhausted by walking up and down the stairs and along the kitchen corridors in search of an apple, sandwich or drink of lime juice, she becomes affected by the phenobarbitone tablets and at last settles down again to sleep. The apparition, in the pink and blue nightgown, is a haunting one — Shakespearean in its sense of doom: her nocturnal walk like Lady Macbeth. But withal she has a hauntingly dignified beauty.

Where this wandering habit will end I do not know, or whether a night-nurse must soon be brought in to help, but it is all part of the appalling *dégringolade* that affects the aged. Doctor Brown says that the restlessness is not caused by her weak heart or her shortage of breath so much as by an inability to concentrate, to remember or know what she is doing.

My mother now seems contented to do nothing each day. She does not read a book or a newspaper. She has little interest in the garden, and even her dog has become a habit. As she sits on the library sofa, she is perhaps remembering things of the past. She has never been one to confide in members of her own family, and has always dismissed as nonsense or rubbish any reminiscences about life in Cumberland where she was born. Now, however, she finds Mrs Talbot, the cook, extremely sympathetic and she also talks freely to my wonderful Eileen, about the hordes of daffodils that were like a yellow carpet under the windows, about how her mother made cheeses that were like butter and unlike any others today. She tells how as a child she would sit in front of the fire with lanoline on her face, or how she would climb trees until her mother warned her that she would be dressed in pantaloons. Sometimes she talks of my father, and of my brother Reggie and what a sport he was. She has become like a child in the house, and I talk to her with the exaggerated kindness and gentleness that I would if she was a six-year-old.

Yesterday I arrived from London and, standing in the hall in my hat and coat, was greeted by my mother saying: 'Are you going?' Sometimes she is amusing. She says in amazement: 'She's seventy-six! Good heavens, she's old!' Given a letter from a stranger who knew forbears, my mother says: 'Goodness, that's going a long way back! I can't be bothered about that!'

DIANA COOPER AND IRIS TREE

Non-stop pressure. 'Don't pay for boat tickets now!' We have no tickets but Diana refuses to give up the chairs from the lounge which she has dragged onto an advantageous position on deck. Stewards fussing. 'Bring the captain. Squatters' rights. Possession is nine-tenths of the law.' An interpreter smiles and tries to prevail on reason. 'We are first class! Look at my credentials. I'm too old to move. Cecil, don't be such a misanthrope. Don't let him take it from under you.' We have to admit defeat when a nicer place is found for us on a higher deck. When we get off the boat I feel guilty. When we walk down the gangplank at Hydra without having paid for our journey, I am ready for the hand of law on the scruff of my neck. But Diana says, reassuringly: 'Well we got away with that one.'

Diana Cooper, having refused all invitations for the Wilton Ball, now decides she'd like to see its glories. But she says she must stay with someone who lives nearby — 'I last longer when I know I can escape.' Since all houses in the vicinity are now full, Diana asks for a caravan so she can sleep in the Park at Wilton. Sydney Pembroke, on hearing this, winces and makes a face as if he'd bitten a lemon: 'I *can't* have any eccentricity in the park!'

Rome

Diana, the beauty of her generation, has become with the years one of the great characters of our time. So strong is her personality that she has countless imitators who try, with far less wit and success, to emulate her 'come off it' attitude to life. But Diana, in turn, has been greatly influenced throughout her life by the Herbert Tree family and by Iris in particular. Iris, the youngest Tree daughter, is here in Rome with us now.

It was the eldest, Viola, whom I first got to know and to worship. She was everything that a young man struggling to break through the barriers of convention could admire. Viola was like a young zephyr, incredibly tall and coltish, she had the quality of a child even when her face became drawn and drab with illness. She was a mistress of the impromptu and a brilliant mimic — but only for one performance. She was never professional enough to meet the challenge of repetition and she could not duplicate some little cameo of observation on the stage. As an actress she was, considering her parenthood, surprisingly ineffective. Having started out with only the highest ambitions, it was sad to see her at the last, in a noble attempt to pay for the education of her sons, having to capitalise on her height by appearing in a grotesque part in a musical comedy.

I loved being with Viola when she came to stay with me at Ashcombe and loped over the downs and drank water from the holes in the tree-trunks. I loved her in Soho when she would go into a grand florist and unselfconsciously buy one long-stemmed rose because that was all she could afford. I loved her answering the door of her Bloomsbury house in bare feet. She was for ever an overgrown child of nature, and it was only after she was cruelly struck down with cancer that I came to know her more exotic-looking sister.

Iris just escaped being an albino. With great cunning she made her whiteness an advantage, and cut her flaxen hair with shears to look like a sort of 'Till Eulenspiegel'. At an age when it was daring to look anything but extremely conventional, she strode about in highwayman hats and cloaks, or in dirndl skirts worn with brilliant flower-embroidered blouses. She became a poet, her life Bohemian in the extreme, and in the many countries where she found herself her friends were mostly artists or writers. She married first the delightful Curtis Moffat, whose unusual photographs inspired me in my formative years, then, later, Count Friederich Ledebur, who is still one of the best-looking, and certainly the tallest, man I have ever seen. For a long time Iris and Friederich lived in a caravan in northern California, then Iris acted and studied in the Tchekov

School in Carmel. Only occasionally would the nomad returned to Europe; but now, for some time, she has settled in Rome.

Iris has a remarkable pristine quality. She never could be spoilt, for she takes nothing for granted. If she is more exaggerated in her manner than Diana it is because perhaps she is the more assured. Both have a fundamental shyness, but Iris somehow makes an asset of what is to Diana and others a great disadvantage. When these lifelong friends get together (they have met only seldom in recent years) they become like greyhounds straining at the leash to run after the hare, so great is their enthusiasm for each other. Not that they gush or enthuse — far from it: they contradict, they argue, but they laugh uproariously and applaud with great glee each other's witticisms and eccentricities.

Throughout these years Iris has never been bored and today, when she turned up at the 'cheap little restaurant round the corner' which Diana prefers, she brought to the occasion a youthful enthusiasm for the pleasure of 'lunching out', of sitting at table and being served with wine and unusual foods. Diana was equally game. Iris was accompanied by a huge dog which suddenly barked and startled everyone in the restaurant. Whereupon Diana shouted: 'I wish he wouldn't do that — it's so common!' (Meaning, I discovered, it is so common to possess a badly trained dog!)

Diana then proceeded to encourage Iris to do an imitation of a colonel whom Iris and her husband once met many years before on an Atlantic crossing. The Colonel had become a figure of fun in their circle ever since. Obediently Iris gibbered like an ape and was extremely funny. Diana's nose screwed up in howls of laughter. The waiter did his usual trick of interrupting. Diana, the chairwoman, in Viennese accent said:

'Come on now — quickly! "Concentrate, choose and order" as Kaetchen Kommer used to say.' 'Wouldn't you like fungus? Or kidney cooked with sage — or those little birds with bay leaves? I won't have them because of my anger at their killing anything so small. But you could have goat — kids — very Biblish and a good taste. Let's get this over! What to end with? Pear and Parmesan? Good! Now that's over! Now then — where were we?'

Diana leant forward in her blue spectacles: 'The Colonel — you were doing the Colonel.' 'The Colonel' started to talk most inexplicably about the Knights of the Round Table. He treated the Knights as old boys of the same club: a hilarious impersonation.

'Now, Iris, do Friederich!'

Iris obliged with an imitation of her husband in a very deep voice: 'Now — er — what — er — time is it?'

'I don't know, Friederich. I haven't got a watch.'

'No, I mean — er — what — er — er — day is it?'

'I think it is Wednesday.'

'No — I meant — er — what time of the year — what month is it?'

'January.'

'Oh, good!'

Iris then scored with an imitation of the Terrys in *The Scarlet Pimpernel*.

In spite of the imperfections that age must necessarily bring and a ridiculous hat she wore today, Diana still appeared to me utterly beautiful. The line of her forehead and nose and the placing of the eye in profile reminds me of a goat, and today she ate goat with gusto.

Conversation now turned to Iris's troubles in having bought a motor-car; Iris admits it was a stupid thing to do since she doesn't know how to drive it. 'It's parked outside only for the policemen to sleep in.' Iris crumples up with distaste when Diana says: 'It's silly to spend money putting to rights a car which you can never sell again because it smells of policemen's feet.'

Iris must be helped. Diana whispers to me: 'Will you change your money at her *cambio*? It will help her.' Iris must somehow have more money. Iris must be encouraged to do du Maurier's *Trilby* in which her father had had one of the greatest successes of his career. Suddenly I became self-conscious for, although Iris is beyond comparison in everyday life, she remains an amateur, in regard to the theatre, even more than her sister Viola. Iris described in long detail her ideas about how *Trilby* could be made into a musical. Diana, sharing Iris's love of this story — all part of their youth — made the only pertinent, constructive suggestions. But Iris droned on: 'Trilby had the perfect mouth formation for a singer: the roof of her mouth was a little pantheon. Her insipid nose should be omitted.' Iris described the songs Trilby should sing — none had anything to do with the plot, or with the entertainment of today.

However, it is part of Iris's rare freshness that she is interested only in the moment and after a while *Trilby* is completely forgotten. In any case she would never put up with the delays, rewrites, slogging dog-work and lifeless repetition that such a revival would mean. Iris savours each second of life too much. The first inspiration is all.

With the years Iris has altered little except that she has changed from a girl to a girl-hag. Her cobweb wrinkles, her sinewy neck, the rough texture of her skin, cannot be overlooked, but her silhouette is the same as when she was sixteen. The clothes are still those of the art student of 1914: huge sweaters, full skirts. Today she wore blue woollen stockings and the same yellow, page-boy bob of her *début*. People stare at her (she is convinced in admiration) as she goes out in her new, barbaric necklace kept in place with a safety-pin. She makes jokes about 'at our age' — a habit which started when she was still young. She had longed to go out and enjoy herself at every lighted candle but Maria Huxley had said: 'At our age we mustn't go out to parties any more.' The joke continued, so now Friederich says to Iris about their proposed trip to America: 'At our age we mustn't go on a fast boat.'

Diana leaving Chantilly

Today Diana bought a house in Little Venice in London. It has been hard for her to decide to leave Chantilly after so long and with so many memories of Duff. Beautiful as her little St Firmin chateau is,[5] it is a witch of a place, luring her to further expenses and complications, needing more and more servants, more doing to the garden, and then, at best, giving the impression of being an impermanent folly.

There are times when the house is not attractive, particularly in winter when visitors are not keen to come. Now that Diana is giving it up, the villa is looking its most beguiling; the weather is putting on its best show and the pale-green blossoming is at its height. But Diana has come to detest the French race, and she says she leaves few friends behind. It is better for her to live on a smaller scale in a city she loves, where she is surrounded by adoring, faithful friends, wonderful family, and many cultivated interests.

---

[5] Her country house while Duff Cooper was the British Ambassador in France.

I arrived at Chantilly for an evening alone with her; I knew that it would be stimulating, but, even so, I had forgotten just how remarkably integrated a character Diana is. She is un-snobbish. She is quick to recognise quality in its many surprising aspects. She has a lively interest in history. At dinner, at a small card table, she talked about Napoleon's humiliation on St Helena as if it were Winston going through those appalling experiences. She was reading a life of Bonaparte and, although she does not approve of him as a character, she feels so sorry for him that she cannot sleep.

Diana has strong feelings about the servants, about her garden, and, above all, about her grandchild Artemis, who was here in dressing-gown to greet me. Diana does not treat the seven-year-old as a child. She talks to 'the light of my eye' as an intelligent grown-up, and pumps her with all sorts of information. 'Who was Medusa?' 'Never say bye-bye!' 'What is seventeen minus two?' She talks to Artemis with complete frankness about everything — including nature in its more basic forms, and about the child's looks: 'You've got a podgy, smudgy face that's good; it will improve with age.' (Her own did!) 'But you must realise your hair isn't good, and you've got to do something about it. Mustn't wear your hair scraggy!'

Part VI: Artists with Paint, 1960

SITTING TO FRANCIS BACON

February 1960

Bébé Bérard did a remarkably fine portrait of me and I think of it as my definitive likeness. It is as I would like always to be. Alas, twenty years have passed since then.

It would be pointless to sit to the usual portrait-painter. But I did like the idea of Francis Bacon trying his hand at me. He had recently done an interesting 'portrait' of Sainsbury, the art collector. The sittings would doubtless be highly enjoyable for Francis is one of the most interesting, refreshing and utterly beguiling people. He is wise and effervescent and an inspired conversationalist.

Francis Bacon has been a good friend for many years now. Graham Sutherland was the first person I heard talk of him, when we were having a discussion on 'taste'. Graham surprised and intrigued me by saying that Francis Bacon's studio nearby in South Kensington had a strong individuality. He described Bacon's penchant for huge pieces of heavy mahogany furniture, and Turkish carpets, the antithesis of all that the painter had once created in the days when he was a designer and decorator of furniture. Graham went on: 'He seems to have a very special sense of luxury. When you go to him for a meal, it is unlike anyone else's. It is all very casual and vague; there is no time-table; but the food is wonderful. He produces an enormous slab of the best possible Gruyère cheese covered with dewdrops, and then a vast bunch of grapes appears.'

When I met Francis we seemed to have an immediate rapport. I was overwhelmed by his tremendous charm and understanding. Smiling and painting simultaneously, he seemed to be having such a good time. He appeared extraordinarily healthy with cherubic, apple-shiny cheeks, and the protruding lips were lubricated with an unusual amount of saliva. His hair was bleached by sun and other aids. His figure was incredibly lithe for a person of his age and occupation, wonderfully muscular and solid. I was impressed with his 'principal boy' legs, tightly encased in black jeans with high boots. Not a pound of extra flesh anywhere.

I don't know much about his background, except it is said that at a very early age his father sent him off in the care of a rider to hounds who immediately attempted to seduce him.

Of his many qualities I admired most his independence. I envied his being able to live in exactly the way he wished, and I was impressed by his aloofness from the opinions of others. We went out 'on the town', but I am not good at pubs, drinking clubs and late hours and would fade away just when Francis was about to enjoy himself.

Recently he came to stay, and although I believe he does not care for the countryside, he could not have been a more sympathetic, appreciative and delightful guest.

Francis began the painting of me two years ago. He had just returned from a winter in Tangier where he had been too harassed and ill to paint. But he was then recovered and full of the joy of London life. He was bursting with health and vitality, in his extraordinarily messy, modest drawing room studio in a most unlikely block of scarlet brick flats in Overstrand Mansions, Prince of Wales Drive, Battersea.

He showed me an enormous black-paint-covered canvas, and said he hoped I wouldn't be alarmed by the size of it but that the portrait would be cut down, if necessary, when he had finished it.

Francis started to work with great zest, excitedly running backwards and forwards to the canvas with gazelle-springing leaps — much toe bouncing. He said how enthusiastic he was at the prospect of the portrait which he said would show me with my face in tones of pink and white. He did not seem interested in my keeping still, and so I enjoyed looking around me at the incredible mess of his studio — a converted bedroom no doubt: so unlike the beautiful, rather conventional 'artist's abode' that he had worked in in South Kensington when I first knew him! Here the floor was littered in a Dostoevsky shambles of discarded paints, rags, newspapers and every sort of rubbish, while the walls and window curtains were covered with streaks of black and emerald green paint.

Francis was funny in many ways, slightly wicked about pretentious friends, and his company gave me pleasure. The only anxiety I felt was that there might be some snag which would interrupt the sittings that were to follow. Sure enough, a telegram arrived putting me off the next appointment; indeed, for anyone less tenacious than myself, there would never have been another sitting.

I went to America, came back, saw Francis once or twice, and he came to dinner, but no mention of the picture from me or from him. Eventually, an opportunity presented itself and I asked Francis if he'd *hate* to go on with the painting of me.

Francis Bacon's name has now become even more renowned. He is acclaimed by the younger generation which, it seems, considers Picasso to be old-fashioned. Francis, bubbling with amusement, smiled and with his usual marvellous manners said nothing would give him greater pleasure than to finish the picture that he'd long had of me in his mind. An enormous black canvas, the only one with its face not turned to the wall, depicted a monster cripple — a nude figure, with no apparent head, but with four legs. It was painted with brushes that had been allowed to slide around in the manner children are taught not to employ. The forms were so gauche that when Francis pointed to the picture and said it was a failure, I was somewhat in agreement. But Francis explained that he wanted more than anything else to be able to do something of that same cripple who had inspired Muybridge, that great photographer at the end of the last century.

Francis showed me a huge canvas covered with emerald green dye-paint. Again he said my picture wouldn't be as large as that when finished, but that all the works for his next exhibition were going to be on these green backgrounds. I had imagined myself as a sort of Sainsbury floating in stygian gloom and wondered what an emerald green picture would look like in any of my existing rooms. I sat on a kitchen chair placed so, and according to instructions turned my head a bit this way. 'No — further! That's it.' Francis started to work with energy, but he seemed to look harassed, not at all happy. I asked: 'Would you prefer if I looked more this way?' 'No — it's fine — and I think if it comes off, I'll be able to do it quickly. The other didn't start off well — but this is fine.' Would I mind his exhibiting the canvas as the Marlborough were screaming at him for more pictures?

Francis works without apparent difficulty and keeps up a running conversation that is illuminating and inspiring. I noticed, among the rubbish of old discarded suede shoes, jerseys, and tins on the floor, one or two very costly art books on Egypt and Crete. Francis tried to describe to me the beauty of two painted figures about three feet tall — a man and woman sitting side-by-side, in cream and white. He said how he longed to take a trip to Assuan later this winter to see the carvings before they are flooded. He thought Egyptian art among the most beautiful in the whole world: 'Those early heads are *amazing*, but, of course, it's because of the sun that they're so beautiful.'

He then laughed: 'You mustn't look at my mouth. I'm just recovering from having a tooth knocked out. My face was in an appalling mess.'

Francis had spent the winter in Cornwall. But it hadn't worked out as there had been such terrible quarrels and he got behind-hand with his work. It was the same in Tangier: such upsets! rows and getting thrown out of the window! He had done no work. Then a talk about Tangier — Francis' Tangier, a close intimacy with the Arab world, with the brothel life, and the freedom that can be found only in certain Mediterranean countries where access to women is difficult.

Occasionally Francis would sit down on an old chair from which the entrails were hanging and which had been temporarily covered with a few French magazines and newspapers. His pose reminded me of a portrait of Degas. He curved his head sideways and looked at his canvas with a beautiful expression in his eyes. His plump, marble-like hands were covered with blue-green paint. He said he thought that painting portraits was the most interesting thing he could ever hope to do: 'If only I can do them! The important thing is to put a person down as he appears to your mind's eye. The person must be there so that you can check up on reality — but not be led by it, not be its slave. To get the essence without being positive about the factual shapes — that's the difficulty. It's so difficult that it's almost impossible! But that's what I'm trying to do. I think I'm closer to it than I ever have been before.'

With Francis the air is mountain fresh: one feels invigorated. I used to go to his studio before taking the train for Salisbury. As the weather was particularly cold, dark and foul, I would be dressed for the country in a very warm, brown suit. Francis was all radiance, even if he said he had been appallingly drunk on vodka the night before. He would expatiate on those evenings: though he didn't really remember much about them, but he'd left an American who had 'passed out' before dinner, gone on to Soho, turned up at his usual 'Club' and didn't know where the rest of the night had gone.

One morning I asked Francis: 'Does it matter my being in a different suit?'

'No — that's a lovely colour. But I want you to put your hands up on this extra chair like this. Anyhow, it doesn't matter.'

During the morning I purposely moved the position of my hands several times to see if Francis would ask me not to change their position. Once he said: 'The hands are splendid like that.' But never again did he ask me to go back to the same pose. Neither did he seem to mind if I moved my head. 'But that's what's so awful about having to sit to Lucian,' said Francis. 'He makes you sit by the hour without moving an eyelash, and I find sitting very unnerving, exhausting work.'

Francis had, during his drunken haze last night, caught a glimpse of Lucian Freud. Lucian had returned from Sweden where he had gone to paint Ingmar Bergman for a cover of *Time*, but there had been too many interruptions for Lucian to produce any result, and he now hated *Time* magazine, Bergman and Sweden. We then talked of Lucian's latest painting — how he seemed, in an effort to paint quicker, to have lost some of his intensity. Lucian was intelligent enough to know that his painting up to now was not a complete expression of himself. He now found himself in the awful predicament of having to try and discover himself again. That, for someone of Lucian's vanity, was a difficult thing to do.

We discussed Lucian's intellectual brilliance, his complete independence and strength as a man who knew exactly what he wanted out of life. But we admitted that Lucian was no angel. After a row, his wife Caroline had said: 'If you want to know what Lucian is like, just see him drive.' Mercifully, Lucian has now been forbidden to drive, for he is reckless at the wheel.

I admitted I found it difficult to be loyal to Lucian all the time. I could not understand the mentality of gamblers, and it worried me that Lucien should lose so much so readily.

Francis said the Bérard portrait of me was a great likeness. (In many ways the two painters resemble one another: both ignoring convention, and living in their own purity — uncontaminated by the asphyxiating cocoon of respectability.) He considered people didn't appreciate Bérard nearly highly enough as a painter at this time. One day they would, since he was definitely one of the great. His use of paint was never thin in quality even if it was spread lightly over the canvas: maybe he had learnt that from Vuillard. How lovely some of the late Vuillards were! And painted with quite a lot of oil. At one time Vuillard and Bonnard were almost indistinguishable, but they went on in their separate ways getting better and better. From the piles of rubbish on the floor Francis extracted a colour reproduction of a Bonnard he had cut out of *Paris Match* and stuck onto a piece of cardboard. The colours were vivid: oranges, reds, red-browns, brilliant blues, enough colours for three pictures. 'I don't know what time of day it represents, or is it night?' With outstretched arms, Francis enjoyed the picture to its fullest. 'You see, people don't appreciate paint today; that's why nobody sees how absolutely marvellous Rembrandt is.'

Suddenly, as he sat, head cocked looking at the picture, his eyes lit up as he said: 'I'm very pleased with this portrait. I think it's going to be all right: one of the best things I've done. Next time you're here, I'll show it to you because it doesn't need much more work on it. When they go well, they go very quickly.'

Francis opened the door, smiled and said: 'The portrait's finished! I want you to sit in that chair over there and look at it.' I walked towards Francis's degutted chair in the corner, not glancing at the canvas on the way. I turned round square and sat to get the full effect. It was as well that I was sitting, otherwise I might have fallen backwards. In front of me was an enormous, coloured strip-cartoon of a completely bald, dreadfully aged — nay senile — businessman. The face was hardly recognisable as a face for it was disintegrating before your eyes, suffering from a severe case of elephantiasis: a swollen mass of raw meat and fatty tissues. The nose spread in many directions like a polyps but sagged finally over one cheek. The mouth looked like a painful boil about to burst. He wore a very sketchily dabbed-in suit of lavender blue. The hands were clasped and consisted of emerald green scratches that resembled claws. The dry painting of the body and hands was completely different from that of the wet, soggy head. The white background was thickly painted with a house painter's brush. It was dragged round the outer surfaces without any intention of cleaning up the shapes. The head and shoulders were outlined in a streaky wet slime.

Francis expected that I would be shocked. He was a little disconcerted. He said it gave him a certain pain to show it to me, but if I didn't like it I needn't buy it. The Marlborough Gallery would want it. I stammered: 'Well — I can't say what I think of it. It's so utterly different from anything of yours I've ever seen!' To me the picture was of an unusual violence. The brushwork, the textures, the draughtsmanship were against all the known rules. Francis suddenly exclaimed: 'Oh, I unearthed these beautiful Egyptian figures for you to see. Look, here they are! How beautiful they are! They're only three feet tall, but the way the faces are painted ...' But what did that signify now to me?

Francis could not have behaved more typically gallantly and charmingly about the fee *d'amis* for the painting. 'Take the picture, and if you don't like it, or your friends object, send it back in time for it to be sold in the Marlborough show.'

I was baffled. Could I ever hang the canvas in any place that I live in? The harshness and ugliness would surely give me a 'turn for the worse' each time I saw it. But I'd gone to Francis for a painting because I genuinely considered him a unique painter. If this was what he felt like doing at this particular moment I must respect it, even if I could not understand or appreciate it. If the Marlborough Gallery would give him so much more for it than he had asked me, then perhaps it would be an investment. I asked him if he'd mind if after I bought it and found I didn't want to keep it, I could sell it again? 'Of course! It's yours to do what you want with.' I took a gulp and said I would like to have it.

I came away crushed, staggered, and feeling quite a great sense of loss. The sittings had been so harmonious; we had seemed to see eye to eye. I had hoped that many of Francis' theories about life, art and beauty were going to be incorporated in the portrait.

No sooner had I written the above than the telephone bell rang from London. It was Francis. In an ecstatic voice he said: 'This is Francis, and I've just destroyed your portrait.' 'But why? You said you liked it? You thought it such a good work, and that's all that matters!'

'No — I don't like my friends to have something of mine they don't like. And I often destroy my work in any case; in fact, I've destroyed most of the pictures for the Marlborough. Only I just wanted to let you know so that you needn't pay me.'

It seemed little to Francis to waste all that work. He seemed jubilant at not getting paid, at *not* finishing a picture. He said that perhaps one day he'd start again, or do one from memory: 'They often turn out best,' he said.

I don't really know what is at the back of Francis' mind. I am sorry that the canvas is destroyed and that there is no visible result from all those delightful, interesting and rare mornings.

AUGUSTUS JOHN

I hated having to take myself out of my warm house. The rain poured in buckets and the windscreen wiper had gone wrong. It was a horrible journey in the dark. However, on arriving in front of the pretty façade at Fryern the dining room was lit up like a doll's house and the scene inside, with the long table covered with food and litter, looked inviting. As always, I was delighted to bask in the rare and sympathetic atmosphere of the John household. Dorelia explained that the curtains were new and appeared too violently red when drawn, so they had to keep them pulled back.

Dodo seemed less worn, less tied down with household chores and responsibilities than usual. She was thrilled that they now had a gardener (three days a week) who was 'making all the difference'. Augustus was in his studio painting by artificial light on some huge murals intended for exhibition at the next year's Academy Show. (I fear they will never be completed.) Dodo sent the Italian servant-boy to fetch him, but confessed her inability to communicate in his language.

Augustus came in holding a pipe in gnarled right hand. As he shook hands with me a sharp pain nearly caused me to shout. A thorn had gone into my first finger — how or why I can't imagine. Perhaps, in a hundred-to-one chance, a splinter from his match had just struck at the right angle. The pain forgotten, we sat talking about Augustus' desire to do a portrait of me. I told him that Francis Bacon had painted me looking like a piece of raw offal against an emerald green background. 'You deserve it for sitting to him,' Augustus said and then, with infinite sarcasm: 'These idiosyncrasies are the prerogative of genius.'

I told him that I had recently read a description in my diary of his being at the Eiffel Tower with a lot of young girls dressed as lesbians. 'I love lesbians,' said John as the door opened to his natural daughter, Amaryllis Fleming, the cellist, a glorious figure of a woman with tumbling curls. Talk then switched to her mother. The triangle of Mrs Fleming, Lord Winchester, and Miss Bapsy Pavry, the Indian, is infinite in its variations on the theme of love, marriage of convenience and divorce.

Dodo is not an easy person to know. Yet she must have realised with the years my enormous admiration for her. Not only am I spellbound by her Luini-like beauty, but I love her calm and dignity. She is mysterious, or perhaps I should say she is one of the few women I've known who possess a sense of mystery. I don't know anything about her antecedents; she is Scottish, she wears clothes unlike anyone else, she is completely amoral. She looks after her hordes of children, and it does not seem to worry her that some are illegitimate. She leads the life of a wife, busy in the kitchen, bottling things, going to Salisbury market; and withal she has a quality so that one knows that she is unlike other women.

With a patience that shows itself in her deep brown eyes, she tends Augustus with the greatest devotion. It is not an easy task. Augustus is selfish, wild and bad-tempered. He loves Dodo, he loves the children, Tristram, David, Romily, Robin, Edwin and Kaspar,[6] Poppet and Vivien — but they are often terrified of their father. Friends and strangers too can be alarmed by Augustus. Fryern used to be like an island surrounded by a dangerous sea. Only the most intrepid visitors were able to make a landing. When I regretted to David Herbert that I had not spent more time in the John colony when I lived at Ashcombe, David replied: 'But they didn't want us!'

With the years, Augustus has become gentler, more mellow. This evening he was positively benign.

I left, full of red wine, to battle my way home through the cloudbursts, with the happy feeling that both John and Dodo were weathering the winter extremely well and that they were in better health and spirits than they had been for some years.

[6] Augustus so justly proud of his becoming First Sea Lord.

PALAMOS WITH TRUMAN CAPOTE

Palamos, Spain: May

One of the pleasures of my visit to Truman at this tiny fishing village was that we could talk uninterruptedly without his being diverted by the activities of unrewarding cafe-society personalities. We discussed the difficulties of writing — he with particular reference to his new work *In Cold Blood*. Truman complained that not more than a few hundred people appreciated the merit of his writing. He was not jealous of the success of hack writers, but it appalled him that his own publishers did not recognise the quality of his work. He felt it was created out of such loneliness, such painful concentration, that sometimes he exhausted himself. His paragraphs were constructed with great care, immaculate punctuation and never a repetition of words or sounds.

Once Truman came to my room saying he had become dazed by a sentence. Did I think it was euphonious? He could no longer tell. It ran something like — 'Still the temperature of the evening had been lowered by the prior incident which had had the effect of making Mr Clutter late for his accustomed bedtime.' Wasn't 'prior' wrong? How could it be simplified? We discussed alternatives; we argued, and all my suggestions were crude. Eventually Truman admitted defeat and cut out half the sentence. After he had left the room I realised the amount of work that he puts into every line. Truman said that the whole investigation of the Clutter murder had been, for him, the most thrilling adventure of his life: that it was terrible, sordid and ghastly in many ways, but he at least had been alive.

During the days on the island Truman and I managed to do quite a bit of sightseeing as well as work. One afternoon we made air unexpected discovery of the house that once belonged to Sert, the Spanish painter of murals. The house was unoccupied, but it still showed the simple yet luxurious taste of its former owner. It was decorated in white — white walls, muslin curtains, white or indigo linen chair-coverings and dark Spanish furniture polished like glass. It brought back to my mind all sorts of forgotten impressions of the extravagance of the thirties. The house was no doubt built with the proceeds from the murals he had done in houses in Florida at a time when they were almost regarded as an essential decoration in the homes of millionaires.

SITTING TO AUGUSTUS JOHN

June 1960

Augustus sent a message through McNamara that he was serious about wanting to paint me and when could we start. The proposal is flattering but somewhat appalling too, for the chances of the picture ever being finished are slight. Augustus must be over eighty. Even at the best of times he was apt to ruin his pictures by going on too long; lately he has chalked up few successes. If only he had asked me when I was a neighbour at Ashcombe he could have done something quite wonderful. For then I was less unworthy of being painted. Instead of this dreary grey creature, I was in the pink of romantic perfection; and I had all the time in the world. Now I work so hard that it is difficult to find time. But in the Ashcombe days Augustus and Dodo were an alarming couple and they did not encourage visitors. Augustus would sometimes come over to me but never suggested my going over to him. Now his two studios at Fryern are filled with discarded portraits and murals. The portions that have not been repainted a dozen times are quite beautiful, but he seems incapable of making up his mind even about the position of legs or arms, and in his indecision, or due to his dissatisfaction, has even taken to embellishing the compositions with silver paint.

Augustus himself realises that he is 'through' — that he cannot overcome the onslaught of old age. Yet the other day Ralph Pitman managed to salvage a portrait of his daughter Jemima before it was ruined. Augustus, although angry at first ('What business is it of yours if I ruin it?') was later grateful; in fact, so moved at having completed a portrait that he burst into tears.

I went over to Fordingbridge in my panama hat and almond suede coat and without more than a glance at me the old boy began to scratch noisily at a large canvas with a piece of charcoal. For an hour he grunted stertorously. He looked like an elderly porpoise staring at me with an expression of desperation in his wild eyes, enlarged by his spectacles. His mouth, under the tobacco-stained moustache, hung open. Every now and again he gave a little jump in the air and landed heavily. His determination to some extent seemed to conquer his inabilities. The first morning produced quite a good, but slight, drawing.

On arrival for the second sitting the charcoal had been wiped into a misty mess, and Augustus started to do another more finalised rendering on top of the original. He took a long time to decide what colours to use; then at last he bashed on a bit of paint. His jargon is 'old student': 'Shall we have a go?' 'Another dodge is to put a curtain there'; no theorising about his intentions and beliefs. Although Augustus has a keen intellect, real understanding about painters and painting and had a classical training at the Slade (where he won a prize for a composition that is one of the school's proud possessions), he is an intuitive painter and he does not, I suspect, know why he works the way he does. It just happened that at a certain time his taste and dynamic strength produced canvases, based on Rubens and sometimes influenced by Greco, that created a shock in the twenties and thirties. Today he is an 'old master'.

I returned next morning and sat without moving an inch for two hours. Augustus liked my hat. By the end of the morning he shouted, 'We'd better stop!', and for good reason: he had started daubing the sensitively painted face with green. Maybe he will right the damage, but the turgid, solid green is of that particularly unpleasant variety that they use to paint cricket pavilions. I realise I have let myself in for a painful experience and one that is a time-killer.

As I drive round the gravel path to his house I can see the old boy, his beret on the back of his head, glaring up at my portrait from his corner of the large studio window. Today he was talking to himself as I went in. It is sad to see this great man in his dotage. The coiled wire of his hearing aid loops like a worm and it seems the apparatus is useless, sometimes emitting a low hum that angers him so much that he flings the delicate contraption to the floor. His skin is pitted with dirt and blackheads, his fingers holding the brush between first and second fingers, the fourth discarded like an old banana, and the palette rattling in his shaky left hand. He spills ash and turpentine on the floor, and his box of matches becomes covered with paint on his palette. Augustus does not notice the electric stove on the floor and falls over it — 'Damn!' He tries clumsily to knock the keys into the back of the frame with a hammer. It is remarkable that he can achieve anything effective under such physical disabilities. His life has become one long struggle against odds.

My portrait continues to make slow progress. I suppose it is taking its inevitable course. But frankly I don't know what Augustus is trying to do. I feel his sense of colour — never his best point — is strangely erratic. One day the green paint on my face is dominant, then the face becomes orange, but when he suddenly finds a very violent blue, he makes this the background for my green coat and pink shirt. It is all very haphazard.

My criticism of the painting is its flatness; it is like a large cartoon or poster.

Today Augustus asked me if I'd been to the theatre in London, and when I told him how impressed I'd been by Finch in the film *The Trials of Oscar Wilde* he reminisced about Wilde. 'I knew him quite well: lunched with him every day for two weeks or more. It was when he'd just come out of prison and he was in Paris. Such a nice chap, so full of fun and a delightful conversationalist. But I didn't think so much of his entourage, and sometimes I crept away. They sat around adulating Wilde and getting him to show off. Who were they? Oh, anybody who'd buy Wilde a drink. He had no money, you know, but he never complained — never about his punishment, never mentioned prison. They'd cut his hair, you know; that was a pity. Yes, he was a bit fat — flabby, I'd say: the skin hung a bit loose. But he was so full of fun. He'd say about Robbie Ross: "He'd defend me within an inch of my life." All the time the trouble was on Frank Harris had a boat waiting; he wanted Wilde to escape. But Wilde said he couldn't face the prospect of being alone on a boat with Harris; anything was preferable to that!' Augustus gave his rich, fruit-cake laugh.

He talked of Picasso — 'The finest draughtsman in the world today' — but when Picasso was painting the *Demoiselles d'Avignon*, Augustus asked him what he was trying to do as he could not understand it. Picasso replied: *'Je cherche la liberté.'*

I look at the accumulation of muck on the window-sill; I see the discarded goblets of milk and brandy (his medicine), the mound of paint brushes. I look at the discarded portraits of the twenties and thirties. I am reminded of Mary Alington, so luscious, so kind, so full of charm; Lord Tredegar, very birdlike and spiky; the Duveen daughter (a brute of a painting, this).

Monday: another morning given up to sitting. There has been, in the meantime, the gaiety, noise and abandon of the party surrounding the Wilton ball. After the long, quiet period that my house has known, with my mother and myself making only sporadic attempts at conversation, the dining room (without its carpet since the storm and flood) reverberated from the stone floor to the vaulted ceiling with the chatter, hilarious screams and yells of six outspoken friends. The ball is now over, but the memory will remain of the Double Cube room filled — but not overfilled — with a sea of dancers watched by the ancestors painted by Vandyck.

Now, once more, back to the picture. Today it was as if every aspect of the picture was closing in on him for attack. He looked suddenly like a bewildered old bull. It was one of his deaf days.

He gave up early. 'Come back tomorrow.' Weakly I said I would. But I warned him that I have only a few more days before I go to the United States. 'I think we can finish it in that time.'[7] He has no sense of time whatsoever. Augustus is great and grandiose, like a figure in the Old Testament. He has

---

[7] The picture was never finished, but was sold after Augustus' death to a tycoon in California.

completely the manner of an artist. He can be lustful and he can drink to excess but he never uses bad language. He is a gipsy but he is also a great gentleman.

Part VII: Travelling Again, 1960-61

STAYING WITH FREDDIE ASHTON

Suffolk: July

The weekend was painfully wet. Fred's sad eyes greeted me from the shade of an umbrella. It was particularly sad for him for this was his only holiday and for most of the time it had rained. I, however, was content to bask in the summery atmosphere of his pretty 1800 Gothic house with roses in Victorian vases, on china and on chintz. The house is like the house of an old aunt or of the girl in *Spectre de la Rose*.

Elizabeth Cavendish was the other guest. We were fortunate to enjoy Freddie at his best. He has become not only portly in frame, but has acquired with the years weight of character. He speaks with great authority and seriousness combined with a frivolous cynicism. He is never hurried, knows his limitations and does not try to do too much. He does not attempt to read many books, but those he does he imbibes with intensity. Things that impress him are never forgotten. Freddie gets on surprisingly well with the common man or woman. He chuckles delightedly when there are family rows and shocking language is used. His eyes fill with amusement: 'It's so human!' When I told him how much I envied him his sense of leisure, he said: 'It's merely laziness. I'm the laziest person in the world: I like to do nothing. When I'm alone my mind isn't meditating — it's merely a blank. I like looking at the ceiling, and when I have to work hard it is just in order to get through it as quickly as possible.'

At dinner on Saturday (a meal which started at about ten o'clock at night) Freddie talked of his favourite, the adored Pavlova. Once or twice he rose from the table to do an imitation, to run as she did, take a pose for the photographer or make an entrance in her grand manner. Despite his plumpness he was able to impersonate the first ballet dancer to make thinness admired; his eyes conveyed his intention so forcibly that one imagined one was witnessing the original. These were moments of real genius. He told us that from today's point of view, Pavlova was technically not a good dancer; that she had no strength, and that half a dozen of today's Covent Garden ballerinas could dance her off her feet. She had poor taste in her choice of composers and in the quality of her ballets; for instance, *The Gavotte*, danced to the most hackneyed of tunes, and *The Christmas Doll* were of appalling banality. Nevertheless, her showmanship was so remarkable that the audience were given the impression that they were seeing more than they were. She might dance for three minutes on end, then take five minutes for curtain calls. She would suddenly appear from an unexpected entrance on the stage, or leap from behind the back curtains, run forward at great pace, or merely subside by the side curtain. He described how the arc-light trembled on one spot while awaiting her arrival on stage. In *The Christmas Doll* she was seen to stand motionless for a long time but, in order not to appear dead and inanimate, she would occasionally breathe enough to encourage the sequins to glint on her tutu, or she would flicker her eyes. Those eyes were magnetic and wild, and were the focal point of a gaunt, birdlike face. In many ways Freddie judged she was inferior to Karsavina, but superior in that she did possess genius.

It was the greatest thrill of his career when as a young choreographer his work had been singled out by her and he was bidden to Ivy House to see the great star.

He was talking to her husband, Monsieur Dandré, in the drawing room when he saw those stretched eastern eyes looking at him above the shutters of the window. She came in. She looked old but marvellously preserved, the skin stretched tight over the bones of her face; and no matter where she stood or sat, she instinctively took up the most wonderful poses.

She took his hands and blessed him. 'You will have great success, one day. It may take a long time, but it will come,' she told Fred. She said that she would like him to arrange dancers for her when she returned from her next tour. She never returned. She had a bad cold, caught pneumonia while changing trains at night and, in those pre-penicillin days, she died.

MEMORIES OF PAVLOVA

Mementoes of former stage productions generally strike one as cheap and tawdry. Rarely are theatrical exhibitions interesting to any but the most eager connoisseur. But in Copenhagen there is a small theatre which has remained unused since 1880 and now houses a theatre museum. The auditorium, the boxes and the steeply raked stage are dotted with busts of actors of the past, their costumes thrown over chairs. The effect is delightful, if slightly haunting and peculiar.

For me, the most touching relics were to be seen in a glass case in the wings of the stage. Here were the costumes, given by her husband, Monsieur Dandré, after her death, that had been worn by Pavlova when she danced in Copenhagen. If we never saw her dance in them, we know them from photographs and statuettes. The best known is the yellow satin Empire sheath for the gavotte, worn with the tall bonnet ornamented with its green leaves, and the gold leather sandals. And here, too, was the three-cornered black hat and the mask that went with the silver and black Venetian costume for the *Coquetteries de Colombine*. Pavlova's dresses in their tangible reality are today ghost-like, without the art that gave them life.

The stage is a world without memory. Often, at the end of a performance, I have left my seat in the auditorium and gone through the 'pass door' backstage, to find that the scenery which a few minutes ago had cast such a spell had already been dismantled, leaving a void. Sometimes, especially in a provincial theatre, I would find that the discarded palace was stacked in the street outside or being loaded onto trucks, while the stagehands were now only interested in the new arrival of the French farce bedroom. It seemed now almost a miracle that here, preserved before us, were the most ephemeral of all garments, belonging to the greatest dancer within our times.

Pavlova achieved her greatest fame as a virtuoso performer after she had broken away from the presiding genius of Diaghilev. But it was then that she was criticised for her poor taste in her choice of musical composers, partners and strange clothes. Diaghilev's designers executed their costumes in sturdy materials of painted linen or appliqué decorations on cloth and velvet. Pavlova would dance as a Bacchante in a wisp of chiffon — very vulgar! Yet Pavlova could rise above everything; Pavlova was unique. Here in front of us were Pavlova's chiffons. For me, these relics held particular significance.

Pavlova had been one of my enthusiasms since that memorable, unforgotten Saturday evening when, suddenly, my father realised that Pavlova's latest season was ending, and that there was only this one last chance to take his whole family to see her. Of course all the seats at the Prince's Theatre were sold except, miraculously, for a box. It was situated very high on the 'prompt' side of the stage from which only a bird's eye view could be obtained; that was better than nothing, and if we were to occupy a box we must all dress for the occasion. As it happened, the cricket match at the Hampstead Cricket Ground, in which my father was playing, continued later than usual. My impatience to embark on our journey to theatreland turned to exasperation with the rest of my family and their last-minute delays.

Long since trussed-up in my first dinner jacket, and in an effort to pass the time, I wandered into the garden. There I picked some of my mother's standard roses which thrived so well in our clay soil; I would take these roses to the theatre and perhaps be able to throw them from our box at the star of the evening. These roses became somewhat wilted by the time they had been clutched in my hot hands during the excitements that followed.

Of course I knew nothing about the technique of great dancers and dancing — could not tell an *arabesque* from a *fouetté* — but my father now informed us we were being taken to see 'the greatest dancer in the world'. I knew from the newspapers that she gave garden parties and danced on the lawn for her guests behind those high walls of 'Ivy House' along the Spaniard's, not far from where we lived on another side of the Heath. But my parents now passed us little snippets about the temperament of the Russian dancer, and regaled us with 'inside' information, widely known, for example that such was Pavlova's rage and jealousy of her partner, Mordkin, that, on one occasion, she had taken a bite out of his ear.

For me, Pavlova was the epitome of all that was rare and mysterious. From the moment that evening when she appeared on the stage, with her big beak of nose, the V-shaped smile, and the long spears of blue painted eyes which gave her the head of a peacock, she was to me the personification of magic. Her fakir-thinness, her mask-white make-up, her stylised, quivering gestures, rather than her flowing grace of movements, sent me into transports.

At the end of that evening, after Pavlova, in the lilac-blue circle of the following 'spotlight', had danced 'The Death of the Swan', she embarked upon the lengthy ritual of accepting her applause. This was one of the great features of all Pavlova appearances and was known to last as long as her actual dancing upon the stage. But on the last night of the season it had extra significance. The more the audience howled its approval, the more the dancer conceived new devices for eliciting even more adulation. She darted off into the wings on one side of the stage, while the audience, under the impression that, by sheer volume of sound, it could 'will' her to come forth from whence she had flown, yelled its delight at seeing the star appear, and rush forward, with arms outstretched, from the depths of the opposite side of the stage. Pavlova then received yet another bouquet of long-stemmed, dark red roses. She reappeared almost immediately in a shower of flowers which rained down from the gallery. The ovation increased until the ballerina was again sacrificed to her public amidst a new welter of magnificent hot-house blooms — no doubt from Solomon's in Piccadilly, that most *recherché* of florists.

The applause and the curtain calls continued. The cheers became hoarse; the palms of a thousand hands were burning and painful, but still the clapping went on. The star figure materialised before the curtains at longer intervals and, though the plaudits were as generous, the flower shower became more of a trickle. Now surely this must be it — this must be the final curtain call of the miraculously revived 'Swan'! Yes, once more Pavlova curtsied slowly, the arms weaving, the eyebrows raised, the eyelids lowered: the tremulous, flickering smile was a tragic goodbye, followed by another farewell kiss to all out there in front. Not a flower was left to throw — except my *roses fatiguées*. This was my moment. In spite of my appalling embarrassment I stood up in the box and threw with all my strength. Caroline Testout fell limply through the air, followed slowly by Madame Abel Chateney. Down, down, down they went, and miraculously they landed at the pointed toes of the *ballerina assoluta*. An electric current ran down my arms, my arms, my spine, my legs. I could hardly believe it when, from among the Solomon relics on the stage, the thin white hands went out to my home-made offerings and clasped my mother's roses. An incredible sense of intimacy went through me. It was as if I had established a sexual rapport with Pavlova and it had been watched by the whole audience. The fact that my family laughed and cheeringly congratulated me only made me feel more embarrassed. But I left the theatre in a daze of fulfilment.

For weeks on end I scribbled likenesses of Pavlova on any scraps of paper lying about our house. The telephone pad was a maze of that precious, birdlike profile and sleek cap of black silken hair. A few months later, at Harrow School, I submitted my interpretations of Pavlova taking her curtain call as 'The Fairy Doll' for the end-of-term competition. When a stranger to the Arts School offered half-a-crown for its purchase, I was extremely flattered and felt enriched. It was the first time I had sold a painting.

THE UNITED NATIONS

New York

A Prince of Cambodia, like a partridge, with a high, feminine voice, spoke in French about his not having as much police escort as the Communists. He pleaded for his country's interests, but in view of greater issues at stake they seemed, to us, unimportant.

After half an hour's boredom, Harold Macmillan rose from his bench to walk towards the podium. There was something about him so cool and collected, so calm and schoolboyish. In fact all the English struck me as being like delightful, hardworking, Upper School fellows, all working tremendously hard for an exam.

The speech was impressive, not only for its oratory but for its directness and simplicity, its understanding, fairness, and wide experience. I don't know if it said anything new from the political point of view, but the entire assembly was deeply impressed by the quality that the man radiated. I was very touched.

It was by no means a conciliatory speech. During some condemnatory remarks about Soviet hypocrisy and bad behaviour, Kruschev, sitting a few rows in front of me, banged his desk with both fists, rose to his full five feet and pounded the air, inveighing against Macmillan. The suave and somewhat tired voice answered the heckling by saying: 'If you go on I shall have to have a translation of what you're saying.' Everyone laughed. A woman next to me said of Kruschev: 'Look at him! He should be put in a cage!' I must say I have never seen a human being more like a bear. On another occasion when he interrupted 'Mac the Knife' he turned round to Tito to continue his vilification of England and suddenly gave the sharpest wink I've ever seen — the wink of a pig.

I was amazed to see how quickly he could turn from fury to laughter. He is a combination of clown, pig and bear. His suit was of poor quality, creased, wrinkled and badly fitting. In comparison, Macmillan in his blue suit, Guards tie and long silky hair, looked extremely gentlemanly.

The influence of Churchill on some of Macmillan's intonations was very marked. The extraordinary, unaffected yet scholarly way in which he pronounced certain words was refreshing. It was heartening and moving to hear his plea for humanity. I came away feeling proud.

GRETA'S SHORT VISIT TO LONDON

November 1960

Greta arranged to come down to the country for the weekend. The visit was curtailed for a dinner appointment. Naturally this did not take place. So she arrived under Simon Fleet's care on the Sunday morning.

Greta did not look as 'downtrodden', to use her word, as I had expected after an interval of nine months. As she got out of the train she was torn between making a demonstration of joy and affection, and appearing self-conscious. She laughed with lowered eyelids. Then when she saw there were no spies she abandoned herself to friendliness and gaiety. She was wearing ski-clothes, a terrible pixie-hat that children wear in the Tyrol, hair now long and fringed. 'Well, well, well, fancy that!' She was in the best spirits as we drove through the autumn tunnels to Broadchalke.

The only anxiety was would my mother still be hostile to her? Last time my mother had thought Greta was taking me from her and there was quite a situation. This time, however, my mother's reaction was wonderfully different.

After an enormous lunch which we both enjoyed, we went for a long walk. There were a few complaints about my being mad to take her where there was so much mud, but she wanted to see (her friends) the pigs and the calves again, and there is always mud where animals tread, particularly at this flooded time in England. However, we walked high over the downs, the air went into one's lungs and made one feel so well. We climbed gates with much protestation and, when it was becoming dark, returned by a hedged path. We had crab-apple jelly, scented with sweet geranium, for tea.

Greta still seems unable to live a full life; she still wastes away her summers in that ghastly flat in New York, traipsing along three streets to get a package from the Health Food stores. Nothing to report of the annual visit to Cap d'Ail, except 'I saw nobody'. She had seen Cecile Rothschild intermittently.

Dinner at Juliet Duff's was sympathetic as old friends were there — Sidney, Michael and Simon. Greta was at her most demonstrative. She looked quite remarkably transformed from the somewhat drab figure arriving at the railway station. She again wore her black ski-pants and maroon sweater, but added a mauve chiffon scarf which was becoming. Her face was animated. Her smile was enough to disarm all criticism. But there was a certain amount of criticism from her of myself.

'You need to breathe fresh air and feel the tread of grass beneath your feet.'

'I know.'

There was a little *badinage* about our getting married even now, but I would not play. I was too sad to think of the waste ...

Greta started to reminisce about her earlier visits here. How we had driven in such cold and foggy weather to London and Oxford. We went through a town (Staines) that smelt of linoleum. How she loved that smell! Once Mr Burton and I had got out of the car, and while we were standing against a wall she looked discreetly in the other direction, she saw a woman walk into the ground-fog and just disappear into eternity.

Many of the things were forgotten by me; things that I had been too busy to remember.

TRIPOLI: COUNTESS ANNA MARIA CICOGNA'S HOUSE

November

One of the rare pleasures of life is to wake in a completely new land and discover the world outside your darkened bedroom. The shutters successfully shielded all light, so that when I opened them onto a huge, white terrace blazing in the sun, I was blinded. It seemed incredible that so few hours away from the darkness of London the sun should sparkle with such power.

I wandered around the terrace looking down onto a white, Turkish courtyard. I climbed onto the white roofs and looked at the distant town with minarets and palmettos. I looked down on Anna Maria's garden — courts with marigolds set out in a lace pattern in a fretwork bed, jasmine climbing a wall and palmtrees completely motionless in the morning calm. This was the civilised Africa of romantic novels that are no longer read, but for which I still have a secret longing. This was a holiday!

It became a habit to walk round the garden at dusk and sit watching the light fade. The variation of light was a wonder. Tonight I sat by the water-lily pond expecting the return of the kingfisher; but he did not come for his evening dip. There were only the frogs and tiny objects darting over the glass surface of the water, disturbing the reflection of the palm tops and the hazy half-moon.

The sunset had been matchlessly beautiful. The slight mistiness in the sky made a mother-of-pearl effect that gave one a start of pain and pleasure. The sun had gone down behind the frieze of palmettos, giving the sky a spectacular orange glow. The palmtrees looked dove-grey and smoky; the white buildings sugary and soft. To walk in this oriental garden was the most perfect visual treat. I wanted to breathe it all in deeply, and let the pleasure remain with me.

VISIT TO ALEC HAMBRO'S GRAVE

Tripoli

He loved Baba. Their course of love was not smooth. He was considered by his family to be unreliable. He had left the Hambros' bank and never stuck to anything. He was sent abroad, away from Baba, for a year.

Baba has enormous strength of character and was absolutely determined that this was the person she would fight to marry in the face of opposition, poverty, disgrace, expatriation, no matter what...

Alec's year abroad only stiffened their resolution. On his return nothing could stop their getting married. Baba had been happy. The marriage had been a success. There were two children.

Now, after all these years — where had they gone? Baba was sending my thoughts back to the past. I felt suddenly very out of context. I saw myself as I walked along with the ridiculous bunch of flowers. I knew I looked pretty eccentric with my large, grey hat on the top of my head.

I suppose any challenge to one's country has to be answered, but the useless sacrifice seems to make little sense. Causes change. Former enemies become allies, and vice versa. But I am glad that there are people who behave with dignity, and maintain a belief even though death is the reward.

'TURANDOT'

New York: January 1961

The first night was electrifying. Never has there been a more charged atmosphere at the Met. The standing ovation for Stokowski's appearance on crutches was thrilling and throughout the performance the audience applauded enthusiastically at every opportunity.

My evening, however, was ruined by one chorus-woman coming on in Act I in the costume I had designed for her to wear in Act III. It was a particularly unfortunate accident as the hundreds of dresses in Act I were specifically designed to be dark blue and other drab colours in order to create the necessary sinister atmosphere. Suddenly this 'trespasser' appeared in an orange skirt, meant for an entirely different scene later on. All eyes were drawn to her. I was dumbfounded and could only hope that she would somehow fade into the background. But no, she was always in the forefront of the stage. When the chorus lay on the floor, the orange bottom was the biggest and most prominent. Then when she went to the side of the stage and stood in an arc light, my rage exploded. I darted up the length of the aisle gathering more fury with speed. I rushed backstage and pushed my way through the crowds round the back of the set until I came to the wings where the orange could be seen in full glow. Here the chorus-master helped me to signal the woman off-stage, although even when the guards indicated with their halberds that she must come off-stage, she moved further forward in the light. Eventually she was pulled backwards. Whereupon, in silent fury, I tore at her skirt. I went on pulling at it in an ever-growing frenzy, but it would not give way. I was beside myself in a manner that surprised me. At last I heard a rending screech of a tear. I pulled downwards in spite of 'Mr Beaton!!' coming from the startled chorus-master. At last the lady was standing in her BVDs with an orange skirt in tatters on the floor around her. Then I rushed back to my stall. But to enjoy no peace. I almost had a heart attack. I sat with my face in my hands completely exhausted.

In the first interval, just as I was about to escort Suzy Parker to have a drink in the Opera Club, I was approached by John Guttman and Bob Herman. 'Do you want the show to go on? Unless you make a public apology to the female chorus, there will be a strike. The Union will close the show!' I was frogmarched backstage. I felt what it was like to be handcuffed and taken off in the Black Maria. I was hurried to the dressing room in which forty angry, half-naked women were changing. A little 'Minnie Mouse' was sitting mopping tears with Kleenex papers rolled into a ball. She wore Chinese make-up and a dressing-gown.

'I've come to apologise for what I did. I didn't know I was capable of behaving so badly. It was inexcusable and I can only say in my defence that we've been working so hard for three months to get the blues just right and to see this orange figure was just too much. But I should never have lost control and I'm extremely sorry. Please shake hands to show you have forgiven me.' The little woman never spoke a word — shook my hand and dabbed away another tear.

Then an angry woman from the chorus said: 'And, another thing, these sandals are all coming apart.' The day was won — Guttman took control of her. We fitted out Minnie Mouse in blue for the last act and, terrified, I returned to the appalled Suzy. For one hour I was alternately overcome by remorse and laughter.

The orange woman had ruined my first night. But despite this I gradually realised what a success the evening had been for me as well as for all concerned. The after-party at Nin Ryan's was unique in that it needed no build-up — all the guests arrived in a state of elation. Noel Coward was adulatory and made a very funny remark about Corelli who is known in Italy as the man of the golden legs. 'Well, I wish he'd shown us his fleece.' Adlai Stevenson said, on hearing of my backstage exploits: 'I've known people get worked up about a word or a phrase. I did not know that one colour could be of such importance!'

Rudolf Bing became human, all shyness disappeared. He roared with laughter about the orange skirt: 'I can't imagine this calm, collected Britisher, this photographer of the Royal Family …'

GRETA

I called her. 'Well, well! I was just thinking about you yesterday. Wondered where Beet would be. Well I couldn't come to lunch. I'm not very well, but don't let's go into that now.'

Nevertheless we did lunch. Greta was in navy blue, a dark chiffon handkerchief on her head. She was smiling compassionately and sadly, and wore an expression of sweetness and childishness. Hers has a quality that no other New York face has.

I am a swine not to unbend completely, not to dissolve into tears; but I cannot. She has hurt me a lot in the past, and I'm resentful of the continued waste, the continued regrets, the lost opportunities sighed over and the new ones never faced.

It is sad; such sweetness and yet such cruelty too, though she would never admit to its being cruelty. When I told her that Mercedes might die (she is to have another brain operation), Greta was deeply upset.

BRIEF ENCOUNTER

The Ambassador Hotel, New York

The telephone rang. It was Larry Olivier just arrived from London at the New York airport. Could he see me immediately? What was I doing for lunch? I was working desperately hard with Waldemar polishing a last draft of my first volume of diaries for an impatient publisher. Waldemar and I had, as usual, planned to have the Room Service bring in a sandwich so that no valuable time should be lost 'breaking for lunch'. For some weeks now I had turned off the telephone and arranged no appointments during the day, and I did not feel now like breaking this routine. I had not forgotten Larry's cruel reception of me in his dressing room at *The School for Scandal* and we had not spoken to one another since that awful evening. What did he want of me now, I asked? He would not tell me on the telephone, but said it was important. I relented. He could come and have a quick lunch with me downstairs in

175

the hotel restaurant, while Waldemar, by himself, would have a sandwich and a glass of milk upstairs.

Larry appeared, looking a bit travel-stained. He was *chétif* in manner, edgy and nervous. He made no reference to our earlier 'situation' and seemed incapable of spitting out the object of our meeting. We were already halfway through the lamb chops, broccoli and mixed salad with Roquefort dressing when I took the conversational bull by the horns. 'What's all this in aid of?' I asked. A lot of flicking of the head, clearing of throat and darting out of the tongue presaged the 'top secret' information that he was going to do a film of Rattigan's *Sleeping Prince* and wanted me to do the costumes for Marilyn Monroe.

I believe Larry was disappointed that I was not more impressed. But when I saw the play in London, I disliked it intensely. I considered the evening's only distinction came from Martita Hunt's quite historic performance as a Grand Duchess — a part in which she had completely eclipsed Olivier and which she was not now being asked to repeat on the screen. I love Marilyn Monroe and would put up with a great deal of trouble, delays and indecisions for this adorable person, and the pre-World War I period is one that I can hardly ever resist, but probably, under the circumstances, this time I could.

I went back to my room and to Waldemar, and we immediately took up where we had left off and worked long into the night. Only next day did I ring Arnold Weissberger, my friend and attorney. I told him to ask the highest fee that any designer in the history of entertainment has ever been given. As I never heard another word from Larry — and not even a thank-you for the lunch — I imagined my demands were considered insufferable.

I felt nothing but relief at having avoided in this manner what must necessarily be a difficult, if not disastrous, association. But the episode was typical of the theatre. On an impulse of a moment, all hands are on deck, everything must be decided upon the instant: don't write, send a wire; better, telephone; better still, hop on a plane and talk direct. Then almost as quickly the enthusiasm subsides; all that has gone before is forgotten.

I am reminded of a story told to me about the Queen Mother that gives another example of her intuitive imagination. When she and the King went for the first time to Canada in 1939 their disembarkation from the ocean liner *Empress of Australia* was a great moment. As the Queen came down the gang-plank, a whole new continent awaited to greet and cheer her. But before she stepped on to Canadian soil, she turned back to the ship's company, assembled to see her off, and waved her thanks to them for her safe voyage.

There are few people in the theatre who remember to look back in gratitude.

BERTRAM PARK

Bertram Park is a pleasant sort of man with an easy manner. He is quite self-confident, knows he does things well, and is immune from the prevalent complexes. He gives himself no airs, is completely at home in the universe, is honest, straightforward, quick, and with a sense of fun. But he is a dull dog.

I have always admired his work and welcomed the opportunity of talking to him at lunch at my house in London. Although I pumped three dozen questions at him about the people he had photographed over the years, I was never able to get him to respond with any enthusiasm. Admittedly his memory for names has gone, but even when I was able to supply these I still got the impression that he had gone through his entire career with only limited interest. He was not able to mention one particular person as being a favourite sitter of his.

He had a few anecdotes to tell of how Violet, Duchess of Rutland, tipped his wife a shilling after she had helped arrange the clothes for her daughter Diana's sitting; and how Queen Marie of Rumania had ordered a thousand 15 x 12 prints of herself. He had been launched originally by Lord Caernarvon, and I imagine had photographed a great number of nudes for his benefactor.

But I felt that he only regarded photography as a commercial business — so many sittings a day to be got through. Yet, despite this, he did produce some beautiful photographs. He thought that perhaps his soft-effect pictures were too sentimental today, but they have taken their place in history.

Today, at eighty, Bertram Park is still in splendid vein, and concentrates exclusively on the growing of rare roses.

TRUMAN CAPOTE

London

Truman Capote appeared at the doctor's where I met him. 'Where can I buy a suit ready-made?' 'Harrods.' 'Right. See you later tonight. Bye bye.'

At Harrods he heard a dog bark. 'Is there a pet shop here?' he asked. He was taken down a corridor that opened upon an emporium that contained macaws, parrots, an owl, birds, cats, lizards and crocodiles and a horrible fox-terrier. Suddenly he saw 'the most adorable, cuddly little bulldog pup you've ever seen'.

He went to an assistant and said to her: 'I would like to buy that bulldog.'

The woman said: 'I am sorry that dog is sold, but we can order you another!'

'No,' said Truman, 'that dog is mine. I wish to buy *that* dog. Here's my cheque.'

'You can't buy that dog — besides he costs £55!'

'My dear woman, I've come all the way from Spain and I know I have been directed straight to that dog. I've got to have that dog. It's my destiny to have that dog.' Truman had not intended to buy another dog after his beloved Bunkie had died, but this was something positive.

The assistant by now looked terrified in the face of this menacing madman. With a backward flick of her arms she summoned Miss Carruthers, head of the department.

'What is it? What's the trouble here?' boomed Miss Carruthers.

'This gentleman wants to buy this dog and he can't; it's a special order and it's been sold to a man who's coming in for it.'

'Of course he can have it,' boomed Miss Carruthers. 'That other gentleman hasn't paid for it. We've been waiting for him to turn up for five days and he hasn't put down a deposit. Of course he can have it.'

Total collapse of assistant. Ecstatic kisses for the bulldog.

ANNE TREE

April 1st, 1961
Anne Tree has real originality, independence and character. She is an eccentric in the old traditional, aristocratic sense, and is often extremely funny when airing her surprising opinions on many sophisticated subjects.

Living in this romantically domed Italian villa in the heart of Sussex, surrounded by birds and dogs, she has a fire for life in its stranger forms. She paints porcelain, collects rare, illustrated books and now, with her zoological interest, has taken up dissecting animals.

As well as running the house and organising her family, she is helping in researches on spermatozoa; in the interests of science her job is to attempt to procure semen from selected birds, either by applying massage to the *vas deferens* or else by putting up a pipette. She describes how the scientist blushes when he tells her what must be done, and also how they roar with laughter despite the seriousness of their work. It is not everyone who can make you laugh over the finer points of the fertility rate of the coot.

NUREYEV

The curtain went up to the music of Scriabin. The huge stage was empty except for the scarlet-shrouded object standing centre. A crack of applause broke from the audience. Here was the exile of the Soviet Union, subdued no longer. Suddenly the cloak moved more swiftly than the eye could follow, and was violently whisked away to reveal a savage young creature, half naked, with wild eyes on an ecstatic, gaunt face, and a long mop of flying, silk hair, rushing towards the footlights. The force and dynamic power of this unexpected figure was shocking and compelling.

The dance upon which he had embarked was so strong in its impact that the theatre became an arena of electrified silence. The wild, fawnlike creature, with the parted pout, was darting round the stage, dipping and weaving like a swallow, then turning in screws like a whiplash. Then he began slowly to weave, like the leaves of water-plants, but always with metallic resilience and strength.

I am incapable of appreciating the intricacies or subtle technicalities of the dance. Even more inadequate am I at describing them. But as I held my breath for fear of disturbing my rapt attention, even I noticed the marvellous precision with which his feet were returned from space to the boards of the stage. The feet, slightly heavy and large, were like blobs of metal attached to a very resilient wire. These legs were strong, but not over-muscular like Nijinsky's; they moved with molten glass fluidity as he made smooth leaps high into the air.

The torso was broad-shouldered, and rather narrow at the waist; the arms were strong and long, and swayed with an ineffable grace and strength. The hands, too, did everything that a sculptor in mobility would choose if he happened to be a master of the ultimate taste and refinement.

Here was something almost perfect in the taste of today. Diana Cooper, next to me, whispered: 'He's better than Nijinsky!' This boy — a peasant until seventeen when he won a scholarship to be trained as a dancer — looks like all the young Beatniks of today. What we were now seeing was the culmination of the development of dancing since it began. Genius is not too strong a word to describe his quality and talent.

Nureyev's wild, Slavic poem came to an end. The audience was for a moment stunned. Then, recovering, it produced its storm of lightning and thunder applause.

The boy responded with charm, dignity and superb Russian pride. He was obviously pleased and touched by such friendliness. His obeisances were lengthy, leisured, and completely relaxed. This twenty-three-year-old creature from the woods was now, beatnik hair and all, a Russian emperor imperviously accepting the acclaim of his people.

When I was introduced to the young fawn at Margot's cocktail party afterwards, I kissed him on cheek and forehead in gratitude.

JACKIE KENNEDY

London: June 11th, 1961

The Jackie evening was interesting in some ways. It was to be the one informal evening in a week of triumphant European official visits for the wife of the American President. Jakie Astor and his wife Chiquita gave a small dinner party for her (apart from the Radziwills, just the William Douglas-Homes and me). Stella, their schoolgirl daughter, rushed excitedly up and down the stairs and backwards and forwards to the window in her nightgown and with one bedroom-slipper missing, because some photographers were outside and knew of their 'secret' guest.

Jackie appeared to be very much an over-lifesize caricature of herself. Huge baseball-players' shoulders and haunches, big boyish hands and feet; very dark, beautiful receptive eyes looking roguish or sad — sometimes they pop too much — mouth very large and generous, with a smile turning down at the corners in an inverted laugh; the suspicion of a moustache, and very black hair.

Jackie's manner is affected, with deep southern drawl. To the word 'marvellous' she would give great weight. She adopts a slight hesitancy which is good because it makes her appear modest and humble.

Jackie was outspoken and impolitic, telling of the rough talk between Jack and Mr Kruschev. Mr Kruschev had said: 'When

I was forty — your age — I was a clerk in an office, and I've grown to be the head of my nation, which shows what wonderful opportunities there are in the Soviet Union.' To which Jack replied: 'I can become President at the age of forty.'

About the flowers and the taste of the festivities at the Versailles banquet, she was ecstatic. About dinner with the Queen last night she said they were all tremendously kind and nice, but she was not impressed by the flowers, or the furnishings of the apartments at Buckingham Palace, or by the Queen's dark-blue tulle dress and shoulder straps, or her flat hairstyle.

Jackie had been criticised for wearing Paris dresses, but she just laughed and seemed to have no fear of criticism. She enjoys so many aspects of her job, and takes for granted the more onerous onslaughts of the Press.

The evening ended early as Chiquita was only just recovering from a nasty car accident, and Jackie was tired too. She laughed a lot when I said: 'When you bugger off, we're going to have a wonderful post-mortem.'

MY MOTHER'S TIREDNESS

July

Mercifully she is in no acute pain, and a lot of the time she pretends to feel ill. But nothing seems to give her pleasure any more. She eats her meals with a lack of interest; she shows no curiosity about the garden or her family. She attempts no responsibility. Everything is greeted with apathy. She is just worn out, and in this condition might last some time more, although almost each evening I fear may prove to be her last.

Mrs Talbot, the cook, has become remarkable as a nurse. Fortunately she has had the experience of looking after the elderly and the infirm, for she did everything for an old man of ninety before she came to us. She is high-spirited and patient with my mother. They get along well together.

Mrs Talbot has said that lately she has noticed a great deterioration in my mother. She is so much weaker, so tired even when she wakes up in the morning. My mother seems convinced that she is on her way out of life. 'Am I dying?' she asked Mrs Talbot. 'What will I look like when I'm dead?' Mrs Talbot, with tremendous resources of good spirits, laughs.

Occasionally my mother does talk to me about the past, about her brother Joe. 'He would have straightened things out!' She talked about how they used to parboil the potatoes then cook them in the oven with the mutton and caper sauce. She tells of how as a child she would go off on a bicycle tour with her father and they would ride for miles — he had such beautiful hands.

AUGUSTUS JOHN

When I arrived at Fryern, Dorelia was there to welcome me. She was, as usual, an almost incredibly beautiful figure in blue and red, with a red scarf draped over her head. Her hair has become grey, her face washed out, but she is still a dazzling asset to any scene. She has the startling beauty that defies the disadvantages of old age.

'Don't know what Augustus is up to but he wants you to go down the garden to the other studio. You know the way!'

I went through the wild garden, past the avenue of Irish yews and sprawling, rambling plants and flowers. Augustus, totally deaf, did not hear my shouts as I entered the room; only when I came into view did he know anyone had joined him. He was sitting waiting for me, sucking at a pipe, with a new square of canvas propped up in front of him.

'This is a smaller canvas, easier to manage. I can do several of you.'

Wild-eyed, trembling in every limb, he banged his brushes on the palette to mix the paint. He stretched forward and dabbed at the canvas.

But the years' deterioration was very marked; everywhere were added signs of weakness. Before he had been able to stand to work; now, as he sat, he jerked and twitched and his breathing became so heavy that I felt his heart must soon give out. Not only was the stertorous breathing agonising to hear, but from inside his chest came other sounds of rusty boxes grinding, of wheezing concertinas and rattling combs.

After a long session of keeping very still, he bellowed: 'Want a rest?' I shouted to know if I could see the picture. But Augustus is completely deaf. No word got through, and he has discarded his deaf aid.

The canvas was the wild mess of a madman. Nothing was there. Just nothing: a weak daub of entrail-coloured brush strokes that fell far wide of their mark.

I wandered about the room. Since I was here last, a dealer had been and ransacked the place. There was nothing left but rubbish and a few old photographs.

However, on with the picture; another session and the blinking old man, dressed like a French servant in blue, bashed away frantically until he said something about tea. I did not want to wait around while tea was brought and made my escape as quickly as possible, promising to return in two days.

The next sitting (and the last) was sad. I watched the brushes flashing up and down. He was becoming hysterical; all the time breathing more ferociously until I had a picture of Augustus keeling over in a stupor. What then would I do? Run for the gardener? Drag him to the door? Or would he already be dead by then? But he survived till teatime.

I sat with Dorelia while we wrote notes to Augustus. But communication in these conditions was very difficult, and after bread and butter I left, Augustus coming to the blue door to wave goodbye.

I know when I am tired how the juice of creation does not come down my arm into my pen or brush. It must be a living nightmare for this maestro who could wield magic strokes suddenly to find the necessary energy no longer there!

August

Quite imperceptibly summer has given way to that marvellous yet sad time of the year, remembered so well from childhood holidays, when the trees were so dark that they were hardly green any more, and one sensed that unwelcome nip in the air which portends the beginning of autumn.

Yet it is still full summer, and it should be a time of relaxation and peacefulness. But it can also be a time when one feels depleted and longs for a more salubrious air. It is the time when wars are threatened.

These last days at Broadchalke have made me feel unaccustomedly melancholy. The reasons are not hard to discover.

It has been my first spell here by myself for quite a long time. Even if I stay for weeks on end there are usually collaborators or assistants working on a play or a set and at weekends a lot of 'neighbourising'. This time I have not even had the company of Eileen and I have been forced to do that which I have always longed to do — lead the quiet life with few appointments to distract me from my painting. Here was the opportunity, but my painting did not satisfy me. It is only natural that having painted so comparatively little, the results of a sudden outburst should not be up to the standards by which I judge the paintings of others. The village children sat to me, and some of these portraits were a little more encouraging, but they did not even make one feel one had earned one's good lunch!

There are times, when one takes stock of one's life, when one feels suddenly much older. One asks oneself important questions about whether one is improving in character or wisdom or discipline as the years pass. These questions have been prompted very forcefully recently by the reviews of my diaries.

Even my friend Jakie says: 'Your trouble is your dancing feet.' Even he is waiting for the day when I will be quieter, can settle down and enjoy a few friendships. 'Don't bother about your ever being an old bore. You won't be, because it's the way you look at life that's fascinating and individual. You have a particular slant and a sense of humour that will always prevent your being a bore, even if you are twice as old as the others!'

TANGIER: BARBARA HUTTON'S BALL

August 1961
The gilt-edged invitation cards summoned the privileged guests for 10.30 in the evening. By 11.30 a hundred ill-assorted people of all ages wandered aimlessly from room to room wondering when the hostess would appear to greet them. The house is almost too oriental in its excess of latticework tiles, painted and carved woods, and divans piled with velvet cushions. David Herbert had arranged a great number of flowers, but somehow

there was nothing to surprise or delight, and quite a lot of the more distinguished, older guests sat around winking or making veiled comments of disapproval.

Trapped by consuls' wives or ex-ambassadors, I revolted. This was not what I'd come to Tangier for. I sought out Ira Belline who, turbanned and bepearled, looked beautiful. She conducted me to the roof-terraces, which were splendidly transformed for the night. In cleverly arranged shafts of light there were scarlet and orange tents. Orange and magenta cushions of Arabic designs in brilliant colours were everywhere. Obelisks, balls and Archimbaldo figures were made of marigolds, zinnias and sunflowers. The effect was made more remarkable by the night scene of Tangier's inhabitants peering from the neighbouring white houses, and in the distance the silhouette of the old town.

Suddenly the hostess was on view, dazzlingly illuminated in a greenish light. The performance was to be given only for tonight. The real emeralds, as big as prunes, were embedded in a great fillet of real diamonds. The egg-size pearls at her neck had an unholy brilliance; her dress was heavily embroidered in diamonds. It was a little Byzantine empress-doll. Her gestures of greeting and affection, her smiles, the look of surprise or delight, were all played in the grand manner. An arm was extended for the hand to be kissed, a graceful turn of the head to greet a Moroccan 'big-wig', a wide, open-armed welcome to an old friend, head thrown back with lowered lids and a move of the mouth — every sort of smile and coquetry.

I watched, as did quite a number of others, as if she was in reality playing a scene on the stage. She seemed quite oblivious of the stares, or of the photographic flash-lights. In her gladioli tent with the brass tray table at hand for her champagne glass, she received the most important Tangerines until, suddenly, she decided to leave her igloo to go to a higher roof to watch some local dancing.

I would have liked an opportunity to talk to her during the evening. But, by now, she was too euphoric to be able to communicate except by pantomime, and to do spasmodic little dances *àla Bali* with neck shaking from side to side, and a wriggle of her shoulders. Standing behind a belly dancer, we watched not the performance but Barbara's reaction to it.

As the evening progressed, she overplayed her role. She was in need of a director to tell her that she was forcing her effects too much. Nonetheless, I was fascinated.

This perfect oval face was seen at its best with the Helen of Troy hair-do and the fillets above. I could not discover why I did not think she looked utterly beautiful. Any minute the curtain might come down for ever. But, meanwhile, the delicate little child's hands applauded, and the exquisite little feet, shod in the tiniest Cinderella sandals, were beating time ineffectually, with tire toes turned in.

VENICE

August

Flying towards Venice in the late afternoon one saw the shape of this small, sea-surrounded town as one never can when living in its labyrinth of canals and twisting streets.

An hour later in the grand Palazzo on the Grand Canal, Brando,[8] my host, said we were all to be taken to the Villa Maser to hear some *cinquecento* madrigals. At once one was involved in a highly civilised eighteenth-century way-of-life that does not exist in many places today. It is probably the last place where footmen in white gloves and family livery help

[8] Count Brandolini.

with the cold buffet of game and salmon, truffles in rice, and wines produced on the estate.

The Villa Maser, brightly lit in the motionless night, came alive as the guests arrived to be greeted by a screaming hostess; a token drink, a *canapé*. The guests were bidden to the terrace to listen to the music against a Palladian background. The sounds created there were of great subtlety and perfection and one marvelled at such exquisite dedication to an art form that, to most of us, may seem rather remote.

The news of a further nuclear test by the Russians, and the sealing of East Berlin seemed rather an empty menace here in Venice where the merits of the latest contribution to film art, *L'Année Dernière a Marienbad*, the interpretations of the Zeffirelli Old Vic production of *Romeo and Juliet*, the exhibition of the Albertine drawings at St Georgio and the modern abstractionists at the Palazzo Grassi were being discussed vehemently. And who could bother about Mr Kruschev when that great impresario, Lili Volpi, was about to give her annual ball?

Lilies were being placed in obelisk form or in garlands; the tuberoses splayed in glass tubs on the floor (*très goût courtesane!*), floral tributes sent by well-wishers. Would the hostess raise her hand to some uninvited guest and shriek '*Sortez! Sortez!*' as she had done in the past?; or perhaps sack all her servants on the spot so that two days later she would be weeping in a completely deserted Palazzo?

Chez nous, the hairdresser in Cristiana's[9] bedroom was attending a scurrying bevy of beauties: Graziella was under the dryer, the Duchess of Alba against her will was having her yellow hair dressed downwards. 'But I wanted it up! I'm always being a victim!' The queue for attention was frenzied, and the

[9] Countess Brandolini.

result was that the other guests assembled for the large dinner-party were all kept waiting. Daisy Fellowes, who, in spite of her weak heart, climbed the stairs with serenity, was now beginning to get fractious. 'I'm hungry. The Rothschilds are always *très en retard*, but they don't mind!'

The motor-boats puff and throttle at the door. The waves lap over the gang-planks, as other boats rush by on the way to the midnight rout. 'If the wind blows my head, I'm done for!' the loud cries are squawked.

A red carpet had been laid on the planks outside the Palazzo, where dozens of husky servants helped the helpless guests on their unsure feet. That social institution, that pillar of all that is decadent, La Maxwell, looked like a terrified buffalo as she was aided to the entrance. She was dressed in gold-bead embroidery of a magnificence that should belong to a Calpurnia or a Volumnia.

The great assemblage was exactly the same group of Venetian society as it was last year and all the years before. All the hairdressers and costumiers had been at work, and hundreds of people involved. Yet there was no note of originality. No dress was outstanding. Only Lili Volpi's beehive hair-do was remarkable in the boldness of its proportions.

She looked bored as she wandered around or sat in positions of abandoned relaxation, leaning on a massive elbow or slumped against the back of a chair. Occasionally she exerted herself to give hell to the servants in the dining room. The head steward looked miserable; any minute his head may fall. She moved a screen in front of the servants' entrance in her own rich arms. She supervises the scene in the ballroom — '*La chaleur! C'est raté mon parti* — the band is *épouvantable!* My silly daughter, Anne Marie, is responsible. I told her this band would be a flop but she insisted, the stupid, stubborn girl.

She's always making mistakes. No wonder her husband has left her! To have married him in the first place was an error!'

The cold buffet was a triumph of the chef's art with huge octopi made of lobster; a gondolier rowing a decorated ham, two bleeding mountains of cascading beef; crawfish filled with crevettes, and pinnacles of shrimps.

Back at the Palazzo Brandolini, where Wagner wrote *Tristan*, a charming scene of relaxation. Most of the ladies have unfastened their waists and bodices. 'At last I'm free! My dress was killing me!' Now they are guzzling ripe figs. The men's shoes are off and strewn about the oriental rugs. The funny vignettes of the evening are discussed. Cristiana says, 'It was a horrible bore. I hated every minute!'

PARIS: MADAME DE HOZ

Arriving in Paris this time I called up the 'past'. 'Oh, Mr Cecil Beaton! [She uses my full name each time.] You will find me an old woman. I'm a hag. You will be shocked, but no matter, come and have a cocktail at seven o'clock.'

The sitting room at the Ritz was surprisingly small for a stay of nearly six months, and despite two abstract paintings, and a few expensive flowers, had no atmosphere.

But the woman in duck-green country clothes who greeted me was bubbling with youthful zest, and I was at once fascinated and stimulated. I had never really talked to her before. (The disastrous time I tried to photograph her a long time ago I was unable to speak French and she had no English!) Now I found her amusing and full of point.

Madame de Hoz is by far the youngest woman of sixty — or sixty- five or seventy, whatever she is today — I have ever seen. Her silhouette is unchanged. The skin is only a little puckered around the eyes, but this gives the eyes more gaiety and melancholy. They are extraordinarily deep-set, like blackbirds' eyes, and together with the short black hair are the only South American traits that she still possesses. In effect she is a fashionable woman 'out of time'. She is not of today, nor is she essentially of any particular time. She is a ladylike woman of impeccably refined taste, never vulgar, but always gracious and totally feminine.

I was beguiled as she sat *en face*, making the situation alive and interesting. She neither drank nor smoked as she talked of life: not with sadness or bitterness, but with amusement! 'What was the life of Paris today? To go to a *bistro*! You ask are there elegant women at the races! You should see them! Nowadays I am the only woman out on the streets who wears a hat! I have some lovely hats from Paulette, but I never wear a casquette or a football on my head. But I can only stand Paris because my husband and I live in the mountains for the other six months in the year, and we are two-and-a-half hours by horseback to the nearest neighbours. The air is so wonderful! You feel so refreshed. You sleep so well!'

'Who is there to look at here? No point in my going downstairs for lunch! So I have most of my meals in this room.' With a chuckle she finds it all a great joke. Even the fact that she is 'gaga' and cannot remember names strikes her as being funny. It is good to see someone surviving in such a delightfully independent, personal way.

Part VIII: Restlessness, 1962

MY MOTHER

Reddish: January 15th, 1962

Generally Dr Christopher Brown has said: 'Physically she's fit, she's not in any pain, she does not suffer. She may go on like that for a very long time.' But tonight this kind, intelligent, very human young man paused quite a long time. Then he said: 'I think you ought to know that she is failing very fast now and it may not be very long before her life is over. I must say she is quite comfortable. Her restlessness is a thing of the past and she is now dozing most of the time.'

The coal readjusted itself in the grate. The library looked very dark and serious. I remembered an incident that occurred just before Christmas. I had been attending to some last-minute detail of the festivities, when I saw my mother standing at the top of the flight of five steps. She looked bewildered at the thought of having to manipulate the further stairs. When she saw me she made a gesture which I shall remember until my dying day. She lifted her arm high and yearned towards me with her thin hand stretching in desperate supplication. All the years of my life seemed to be cast away as I ran towards her and tried to give her the support that she had given me as a child.

January 23rd

Somehow or other this slow process of dying was different from what I had imagined it to be. Death has always seemed sinister — it had elements of cruel mystery, something to be ashamed of. This was sad, but no more frightening than the crumpling up of a flower, or the weakening of a bird.

She scrutinised her hand a great deal and seemed surprised that her wedding-ring now slides loosely on her fingers. She likes to have me sit by the bed holding her hand. She looks very beautiful.

February 23rd

I had to go to Paris for two hectic days of work. It was at the end of the second day that at last I lay down on my bed at about 6.30 in the evening. The telephone bell rang. Since we had already discussed all the business in hand, I was surprised that it was Eileen. She told me in a very calm, off-hand way that my mother had died at 3.30 that afternoon, that it had been most fortunate that Nancy had been with her, also Mrs Talbot and Doctor Brown; that she had died very simply and quickly — no pain — very peaceful. I took the news so calmly that I could only wonder at my lack of emotion.

I knew that my mother's death was a relief, that it was something we had even prayed for. She was no longer anything but a living anxiety to herself and to us. Now that it had happened, one remembered the past, the difficult times and the good times. I remembered so many of the incidents from my earliest days. The snapshots of my mother in 1902 fashions with wide sleeves and upturned hats, dangling me on a knee in a hotel sun-lounger or on the sands; the snapshots in the little front garden with its black and white stone path; the baskets of geraniums, and the string-laced green blinds at Langland Gardens. In such a long life as hers — she was born in 1872 — the snapshots filled many albums, from the time that she smiled coyly as my father's affianced, to the sad time when with wild, white hair she sat impatiently on the terrace.

I remembered the wonderful, soft kindness of her welcome. There was something about going back to her protection that was different from anything in the world.

One of one's greatest early childhood pleasures was to be allowed into her bedroom, and to snuggle up close to her in bed, while she read her letters, and made all life seem sweetness, kindness and happiness.

My childhood was idyllically happy, with occasional dramas of a sudden thunderstorm during a picnic, a musician *almost* getting drowned while bathing, a case of scarlet fever, and the annual exodus with hold-alls and a hip bath. My mother soon after arrival at the seaside was always struck with a sick headache.

These early years were almost cloudless. There were jokes about Daddy putting on uniform in the 1914 war, and, when meeting someone unexpectedly, doffing his cap instead of saluting; there was the excitement of coming down, wrapped in a rug in the middle of the night, during the Zeppelin raids.

But it was only much later that things started to go wrong. My mother seemed vaguely worried that Daddy complained about business not doing so well, and after we had moved from Temple Court, where all was halcyon, and arrived in Hyde Park Street, troubles were combined with miseries and anxieties; then my brother's death, which affected my father so grievously; and then my mother was my responsibility. Sometimes we quarrelled, as is only natural with two such strong characters living in close proximity. My mother could never believe that I had ceased to be a child.

I rushed out into the garden, and blubbing like a fool, walked up and down the lawns in the cold air. I wanted to die of my grief. After a time Nancy came out and, her arm in mine, told me how marvellously peaceful the end had been; how fortunate that it had been so painless and dignified. How Mummie had given Nancy two seraphic smiles then turned on her side, and breathed like a child, and then no longer breathed. 'You must go and see her. There is nothing frightening about it. She looks beautiful.'

Mummie lay in her darkened bedroom very low in her bed. I was surprised to see how small she was; her head had been tied with a white cloth under the chin. On her chest Nancy had put a little bunch of flowers that she had picked from the garden-pink azaleas, violets, snowdrops, primroses and jasmine. She looked vulnerable and trusting. Her forehead was so cold. I hurried from the room.

I could not wait at the church lychgate after the Broadchalke service for the usual politenesses — the shaking hands, and commiserative smiles. I bolted. I rushed back shivering to my bed, and remained in a daze.

MY MOTHER'S FUNERAL AT HAMPSTEAD

March 2nd

West End Lane looked very small. The single line of traffic made progress very slow today. The funeral-parlour chauffeur drove with extreme caution; even the windows fogged up and my black-gloved hand wiped the steam off the window, the better to see the well-known landmarks.

The shops that I remembered from childhood had long since passed into other hands. Once there had been a shop that contained a wonderful revolving picture-postcard stand, with rare pictures of my favourite actresses; a nice sweet-shop and a dry cleaners with a beaded evening-dress in the window; and I noticed a great number of fruit and vegetable emporiums with huge pyramids of oranges and apples. Outside another, a dark, burly young man was unloading sacks from a truck. The snow was coming down so fast that his hair became white, and he had to shake the snow from the sacks before taking them into a bird and tackle shop which also advertised 'cat boarding'.

On arrival at the cemetery the snow was deep. Some brightly coloured wreaths lay by the porter's lodge. We drove on slowly. Nancy and Hugh Smiley had arrived from the country and were visible as they waited behind the steamy windows of an overheated motor. We progressed in the motors a few hundred feet and waited. There was no message to say that the hearse would be late, but the snowy journey from Salisbury must have delayed matters.

The clergyman was waiting by a chapel. A few old, red-faced gravediggers hung about. We looked at the acres and acres of Victorian and Edwardian tombs. Sorrowing angels with rose garlands mourning an elderly couple who died in 1889 and 1896. Some of the 'last messages' were unfortunately phrased. 'She was the eyes of the blind, the feet of the lame.' The snow was falling in heavy flakes onto granite crosses and obelisks. It was so white that the sky seemed khaki-coloured.

The last journey. My darling mother was brought, under a purple velvet pall and our lilies, to her last bed. We followed to the family vault. We stood, a forlorn, black, family group. The clergyman, with a very red nose, was reading the last prayers. We were sad as the gravediggers, banded together, moved the coffin towards the grave, then slowly lowered it into the Beaton tomb. A kindly-looking old Shakespearean dropped a handful of earth onto the coffin, and we encroached very slowly to look our last. Nancy threw a little bunch of snowdrops onto the coffin. I saw my mother's name engraved on a brass plate, and beneath this coffin was another one, mouldering with age, possibly the coffin containing the remains of my father.

Baba, who is generally so calm and self-contained, whimpered and was comforted by Nancy, whose complexion in the intense cold was dazzlingly pink and white. We looked at the flowers. The snow made our lily cross look dark-ivory coloured, but some kind friends had sent some carnations and they were a bright spot in this bleak Giselle scene. We got back into the two motors and, leaving our mother to lie in the cold earth, we returned to our everyday life.

NIGERIAN INTERLUDE: THE 'SALLA' AT KATSINA

Northern Nigeria: March 1962

Just as music can create certain sensations, so here, by the unexpected effect of the use of black, scarlet, blue or purple, colour creates a vital emotion. How can one explain that even pale colours create a shock of pleasure, violent and deeply overwhelming? Polo ponies are dyed carrot-pink; a horse is covered with a cloth of lettuce-green; a whole army wears magenta, or wasp-like stripes of orange and black; a turban like a cloud of peppermint. There is no apparent method in these groupings of colours, but somehow they combine to form a picture which is totally African in flavour, and produces, in the spectator, a state of elation.

The Emir of Katsina is holding the *Salla*, which celebrates the appearance of the new moon and the breaking of the thirty-days fast of Ramadan. The variety of different materials used in this splendid spectacle range from embroidered cloths and silk from Damascus to fabrics of cotton from Manchester;

silver thread of the eleventh century is surprisingly used next to a Victorian rose-budded chintz; butter muslin is combined with cloth of gold, brocade and tinsel are mingled, and the shine on the aubergine-coloured turbans is produced by an almost endless knifing of the leather.

The Emir has passed in procession through the fourteen gates of the city to the prayer ground. Here, guarded by his two war leaders, the *Auraka*, with unsheathed sword held aloft, he has given thanks for the benefits his people have continued to enjoy and is now returning to receive their homage.

In the far distance the drums can be heard by the crowds bordering the big square at the gates of the Palace. The *tambari* (tambourines) are beaten only in the immediate presence of the Emir, and they produce an excitement among the pale blue-and-white-clad population that has to be kept in check by police equipped with whips.

A huge bronze figure in white, scarlet and emerald (the Court Jester), shouts his lungs out as he introduces the entertainment about to be enjoyed. The open square is invaded by hundreds of laughing boys weaving and twirling upon bicycles like the clowns that somersault into the arena at a circus.

It can now be seen that the drums are being beaten by frenzied drummers mounted on camels, and haunting sounds issue from the long ancient metal horns being blown by musicians with melon-fat cheeks. The brass hats and tall black feathers of the Emir's personal bodyguards are worn with chain mail armour that goes back to the time of the Saracens. Their richly caparisoned steeds are weighed down by elaborate harnesses trimmed with scarlet and yellow tassels.

Then on foot come the beautiful scarlet and viridian cotton-clad army of the *Dogari*, the watchmen, who, together with the archers or men-scouts, flank the Emir on all sides. Their emerald and pale-green uniform originated as camouflage in the jungle. Violent, warriorlike women, with startling black head-dresses, lurch flat-footed while brandishing ferocious knives and cutlasses.

Under a huge, whirling, red-brocade parasol, in a din of music and song and wild cries of fervent admiration, trots the smiling Emir. As leader of his people he is suitably dressed in modest white.

When his white stallion reaches the end of the great square, the ruler halts, turns, and then proceeds to watch the *Jasi*. This is the display of horsemanship and bravery enacted by his loyal supporters who have come from all parts of his Emirate to show proof of how brave they would be in support of their Chief in time of war.

The *Jagi* (the Master of the Horse), in gold tunic and huge red turban, rushes around in harassed, Alice-in-Wonderland fashion to stage-manage the details. Suddenly, horsemen emitting wild cries, wielding aloft ferocious long spears, gallop forward in a cloud of dust to within a few yards of the Emir. Precipitously, they turn, then, amidst a storm of applause, give way to the next charge. This is not a commercial make-believe, or a film. It is part of a real fairy story that has continued and survived since the Crusades.

After an hour's display of skill and daring, speed and control, demonstrated with a casual bravado, the *Jasi* is over. Now the populace, so long kept at bay, in one wild rush burst from all sides to fill the square. The dust-storm thus created settles, to reveal thousands of massed heads looking like caviar of opals and black seed-pearls.

The Emir delivers a speech to his people. He advises them to be active in growing crops and maintaining the cultivation of the land by which they live. They must not neglect to fertilise the earth, and he warns them not to relax in their fight against meningitis and disease.

When at length the Emir retires to the private apartments in the compound, it is to witness a family demonstration of the loyalty, affection and love of his more immediate dependants; the womenfolk, servants and wives of menservants of the Palace, do war dances and scream with joy. The scarlet archers dance in circles with swords: they are said to have eaten certain medieval herbs which have made them immune to cuts by metal, knife, axe or arrow. They shriek war-cries and proceed to carve with sharp steel, in a frenzy of enthusiasm, even their most delicate parts.

The Emir realises the humour of certain situations and throws back his head in guffaws. He is enjoying his day of ceremonial and avowal of faith.

For all of those who live under the stress of modern civilisation, with its onslaught of noise, smells, commercialism, ever-increasing speed and refinements of killing, and for all those conscious of the Damoclean sword of nuclear war, a visit to Katsina is in the nature of a return to sanity. This is something that the human mind can comprehend. Katsina has always been noted for its learning and culture, and has attracted people of all nations since 1100, when it became the centre for the caravan trade with the Mediterranean ports. Today life seems easy. There are no signs of painful poverty. Prayers are said in thankfulness for continuing peace, but also that if battles must be fought they shall be feats of bravery, daring and horsemanship.

DINNER WITH JULIET DUFF

Wiltshire: April 14th

Juliet is not having a holiday this August. 'I've had so many expenses. The wall fell down in the kitchen garden and the greenhouse needed repairs, and we had to have the hall recarpeted because of the dog stains. Everything costs so much that we've had to send a bit of jewellery up to Sotheby's.'

In spite of her strong personality, she is a weak character, gutless and apt to change her opinions according to those of others. But the fault that has increased with age is her scattiness.

Tonight Juliet was on her mettle as Lady Churchill was staying for the weekend; Raymond Mortimer was there too. Like the Edwardian hostess that she is, Juliet was determined to stage-manage her little party and to give her chief guests an opportunity to shine. Somehow she managed only a few interruptions, but these were easily parried by Lady Churchill who is a good talker and accustomed to holding the stage.

Clementine Churchill told us about her friendship with Walter Sickert whom she knew first when she was a gangling, fifteen-year-old schoolgirl at Dieppe. She said that he was a most wonderful-looking man, living in lodgings that were owned by a Madame Villain, who had several children running around with a marked resemblance to him. But of course as a schoolgirl she had no idea that the rather possessive housekeeper was anything more than just that.

'Which is Mr Sickert's room?' the young Clementine had asked.

'He's out!'

'But he asked me to come and see him!'

The landlady smiled in an enigmatic way. 'You can go in and see if you don't believe me.'

The bedroom that confronted the visitor was in an appalling state. The bed had not been made; there were unattractive sights under the bed; and there was a fish skeleton on an old plate on the windowsill. Clementine described how she cleared up the room; she made the bed, covered it with a counterpane (pronounced 'counter-pin') and with delicate fingers tossed the fish remains into a convenient dustbin which she found outside the window. When Sickert came back a little later he was not at all pleased to find that his '*nature morte*' had been destroyed.

Sickert had never painted his ardent young admirer, but once, when she arrived red-faced and radiant from a hockey match, he took a red-hot poker from the fire and burnt on wood a caricature of her, thin and beaky-nosed, with the hockey stick. 'That is to show you how you look.' 'It was a most excellent likeness,' the sitter conceded.

Four years later the young girl was told by her mother that she could go to Paris with her governess and stay as long as they could on £25. By eating little they managed to stay for two weeks. While they were there Sickert called most unexpectedly one morning at eight o'clock, with a bag of brioches, to take the nineteen-year-old girl out to see Paris and some pictures. (The governess was delighted to have the day off to visit relations.) Sickert and Clementine went to a cafe in the Champs Elysées for breakfast of beer and brioches. The beer was not paid for, but marked up as being another debt that Sickert owed.

Sickert appeared to have no money, and they walked everywhere. First to the Louvre, where Clementine was asked which was her favourite picture. She pointed out Sargent's *La*

Carmenita. 'That shows your bad taste,' said Sickert. 'Now look at this Puvis de Chavannes!'

'Oh well, that's a classical picture,' retorted the defiant girl. From the Luxembourg gardens they walked all over Paris until past lunchtime. Again Sickert was not able to pay for their meal, and a chalk mark was put up on a board.

'Now I'll take you to see someone you'll never forget,' and together they went to visit Pissarro, who sat wearing a large black hat, surrounded by his enormous family. As the night approached, Sickert said: 'And now I'll show you a fashionable painter,' and, wisely enough, they dined with Jacques-Emile Blanche, for he provided excellent food and wines.

The young girl's infatuation with Sickert did not burgeon. Later in life the two seldom met, and she grew to have rather a poor opinion of the great man for 'He was, I think, without doubt, the most selfish human being I've ever come across.'

PARIS

May 1962

The experience of working on *The School for Scandal* for the Comédie Française has been in great contrast to some of the jobs I've had in the theatre on Broadway and even in London. Each department is headed by an artist, someone who understands the difference between thirty different colours of grey. The tailor spends a morning finding the right silk for a lining or button for a waistcoat; the wig-maker spends infinite time annotating one's wishes; and the head of the scene painting says, 'You must be sure and tell us if you're disappointed with the work and think it should be done with more refinement.'

As for Karinska, to work with her is to feel that it is easy to design and make beautiful costumes.

Raymond Gerome was always so calm and polite I found it hard to understand that excellent work could result with a display of so little temperament.

As for the authors, Barillet and Gredy, they were enthusiastic and sometimes critical aids to a final effect, and the Administrator, Monsieur Escande, gave forth a flow of gracious compliments that could not fail to gladden my heart.

It is a delightful world of creativity and my last three visits to Paris have centred around those descendants of the seventeenth-century theatre who work in those eighteenth-century attics by the Palais Royal, doing the classics as if for the first time. My new Paris celebrities are M. Chaplain, the *perruquier*, who smells strongly of fish after lunch, his wife, with her white Gainsborough Pomeranian lying by her side as she works through thick glasses on a front piece of hair; the head cutter, Ernest, with feminine hands, who lovingly smooths a perfectly cut hunting coat; and Mr Hoff, in charge of the stage.

Food of all sorts is expensive enough in Paris, but the fruit is so reasonable in quality that one does not mind paying for a pear or an apple as if it were a jewel. I ordered eight pears and while they were being packed up was able to admire to the full the marvellous display of fruit on counter and window. This year spring has been particularly late in appearing and this made the 'out-of-season' fruit arrayed in tiers seem even more remarkable. There were enormous, globular bunches of pale-green grapes, wonderful symmetrical pale-green artichokes, ceps of all shapes and colours, heavy custard apples, mangoes and aubergines like bolsters. Even the oranges and tangerines not only tasted better than all other oranges and tangerines but looked as if they did too. Passers-by outside would stop and smile as they gesticulated at the marvellous sights, the most remarkable of which were the two boxes which contained half-a-dozen bright, ruby red strawberries that were as big as fir-cones.

The fruit and vegetables in this shop are treated with the care which they deserve, and the white-haired duchess who attended me arranged that my pears should be beautifully wrapped for the aeroplane. The procedure took a great deal of time. While I waited my gastronomic juices were working overtime as I admired the best of every sort of sausage, pate and cheese. It was a busy time of the morning and there was quite a *va et vient* in the shop.

Suddenly an old, old woman, all in black, a black shawl over her head, and carrying in one gnarled hand a large, cracked black leather bag, appeared in the doorway. She was the very essence of old age and the essence of France. Everyone in the shop watched her and was for a moment quite quiet. Whether the lull was created by shock or embarrassment I do not know. The ancient woman hung for support onto the glass of the door. She was bent forward and her face was solid and pink; although not particularly lined one knew she was ancient; she must in fact have been eighty-five years old. But although she looked healthy enough, she had outlived her strength. She knew she could move only with great care, and the effort of coming into this shop was almost more than she could manage. Yet the habit of a lifetime is strong, and she knew instinctively how to preserve herself from falling. She stood peering with a dazed gaze into the interior of this grand emporium.

One of the assistants called cheerfully, '*Entrez Madame*, and gave the old woman a present of some appetising meat and wrapped it in shiny paper. The old woman could not say thank you, she merely stared with large, incredulous eyes peering from her rosy, rough-hewn face. She had a drop at the end of her nose, and her stockings were twisted round her 'shrunk shank' like a gnarled tree. She was like all the French peasants one has ever seen; she had the earthy ruggedness of Van Gogh's early paintings.

I wanted her to know how friendly we all felt towards her, and so I stood meeting her bewildered gaze with a forced smile on my face. But she did not understand anything. Another assistant ran to put a large tangerine in her cracked old bag, and I managed to put a coin in her hand. Lurching forward, she slowly turned with enormous dignity towards the door again, to take herself out into the bustle of the Madeleine. She was shockingly old, and one felt how near to death she must be.

GORDON CRAIG

South of France: May 24th

His refuge high on the hills of Vence was hard to find, even with the very specific instructions I was given. However, eventually, Indian-inked signs and arrows marked on trees showed the way to the back of the shack in winch Edward Gordon Craig, aged ninety, fives, cared for by one of his daughters.

The shack was shuttered tightly. I feared my luck was out. I knocked hard and repeatedly, then I heard sounds of movement within. After a bit a pale, blue-eyed, frizzy-grey-haired woman appeared. She gurgled an English sentence in a deep musical voice. I gave her my name and asked if I could see Mr Craig. Her smile became very forced as she looked at my camera and said: 'But I don't think he'll want any photographs.' I called for the driver to take my camera back and waited, as bidden, on a garden chair. Eventually, cackling and high-spirited, the old colossus appeared. He was like a huge bird that had lost many of its feathers. His nose was a beautiful beak, his mouth was toothless, and the long strands of pale cream silken hair were a bit fitfully placed on his scalp. He wore a high, white Regency collar with old, rather wintry clothes, a woollen coat with many of the buttons missing and baggy trousers, with the knees patched with some brown flannel. His flybuttons, or rather his zip, was discernible. He wore thick shoes, similarly zipped. The effect was untidy, artistic, but not dirty. There was, in spite of his age, something rather immaculate and healthy about him. He was immensely tall in spite of a hunch, and waggled all over like a sheep dog that is pleased to see a friend.

'You want to take a photograph? Splendid! You're the master. There's only one like you. How do you want me to be?'

The driver brought back the camera and within a minute the old bird was posing in a most felicitous patch of light that came through a small window in the corridor.

His daughter gurgled musically: 'Oh, and with all your buttons undone?'

The old man shook off the admonition: 'What's it matter? We're beyond all that!' was his gay brushing aside of all but the important tenets of behaviour.

'You must have known lots of my friends — Max Beerbohm and Rothenstein. I've often wondered when we'd meet, and here you are! Oh, I like the way you take photographs. You're a genius. I can see that. You're the most unprofessional photographer I've ever seen at work — but that's good. I can see you're interested and I like this. This is splendid!' He chuckled with glee.

'Where's my hat?'

The daughter fetched a big-brimmed, felt sombrero that made its owner look like a lesbian. Cackle. He posed with arms akimbo and then looked up to the ceiling like a saint in ecstasy, his pale eyes lively and quick through his spectacles. I clicked away with fervour, almost surprised that even without any preliminary talk we should so soon be involved in this ritual. Within a few more minutes I felt I had achieved as good as I could possibly get, and we moved into his small, book-lined den. He sat at his desk and, in spite of his deafness, was able to carry on a conversation. Occasionally the daughter would repeat in his ear some remark that I had made. There seemed to be a marvellous rapport and love between the two of them.

The self-sacrifice of the daughter had brought her an inner peace that one could easily recognise. Living a hermit's life, acting as Cerberus, she was not for one minute bored looking after this old man.

Her eyes brimmed with goodness and affection and her father said: 'Daughters are the thing!' This reminded me of a line of Barrie's in *Dear Brutus* — but Craig had always hated Barrie. 'He was such a beastly man — so mean and despicable!'

'What can we offer him to drink? Champagne?' he said rather surprisingly. The daughter said they also had whisky and brandy. 'I'd love some water,' and she brought in a bottle of some mountain spring water that was cold and delicious.

I was fraught with excitement at meeting, at last, a great figure of the theatre that I'd heard about since my earliest, stage-struck days. When I mentioned my admiration of all that he'd done in the theatre, he threw it aside as beyond speaking about.

'They never did any of my things. Cochran was going to, but everything fell through. I've never had any luck in England. They know me much better in Switzerland, Poland and Russia. I know very few English actors. They're not an interesting lot. Bernard Miles is an exception. He comes to see me three or four times a year. What he does is interesting. But I don't like actors. I was an actor once, but not for long. It's funny, but I never knew my father except when I was very small, perhaps five years old. But I've never forgotten him, and he has meant more to me than anyone else in my life. Here's his photograph dressed as a monk. He was always dressing up, but he wasn't on the stage.'

Craig chuckled. 'I've sold a lot of my books to the Bibliothèque Nationale in Paris, but [*with a wink*] by no means all!'

He is a bad businessman and could have sold his books at a much greater profit, but he knows he still has a nest-egg in his possession.

'Here's a nice book.'

He opened one or two leather-bound volumes from which the innards had been torn and inside were little playlets in Latin or Italian which he had bound himself. Arty and useless I considered, but to Craig they mean a great deal.

Craig was game and courageous and seemed perfectly contented, though, as a sort of act, he pretended to be angry at being marooned so far from play or film; without a telephone, without a car. To me it was nevertheless rather a pitiable picture; there is something so tragic about old age that I felt it an impertinence of a stranger like myself to come and eavesdrop.

LILY ELSIE

June

Lily Elsie, the heroine of my youth, has died. Her last years were spent at St Andrew's Hospital, Dollis Hill, where she was extremely happy in her anonymity. She had occasionally been taken by friends for a ride in a motorcar and to have tea at Henley or Hampton Court: she had praised the *pâtisseries* at Pinner.

'The bones hold my face up,' she had said when a friend told her that she was as beautiful as ever. Although she had always disliked being 'recognised' in public, she was not displeased when one morning her Australian nurse ran in and said: 'You never told me you were a movie star! The man in the next room has a collection of picture postcards and all of them are of you.'

Lily Elsie's success in *The Merry Widow* at Daly's Theatre in 1909 made theatrical history. Cecily Webster, the last surviving member of the original company, remembered her on the first night waiting for her final entrance in the third act. The house had cheered itself hoarse and were in a state of ecstatic hysteria. Lily Elsie, with the typical modesty that was to remain with her all her life, turned and whispered: 'I think they like us!'

King Edward VII saw *The Merry Widow* four times; people from all walks of life became devotees, and it ran for 778 performances. She will be missed by many people who are still attuned to *The Merry Widow* waltz, and I shall always remember her.

August 3rd

After the Comédie Française job, which was a delightful departure, as the Americans say, I returned to a long, frustrating period trying to get Pelham Place redecorated. I tried to paint and made no progress. I longed to 'stay put' in the country, instead of always having to come to London for two days of exhausting, crowded appointments.

There are things moving (the film *My Fair Lady*) which may save my financial situation but will not help the real cause of my trouble, and the more difficult years are looming. There are no real alibis. Time ferrets out all the weaknesses, and they become ever more apparent.

CLARISSA EDEN

Broadchalke: August 5th

Clarissa Eden had to come to Broadchalke to meet Mr Blick, the builder, about the new water supply going up to her cottage. She arrived, her hair in a late thirties bob.

The rain stopped and we made a brief tour of the garden.

'Where do you get that curry plant?' she asked the gardener. 'Do you go to Murrell for all your roses?'

When we came back to the house it was a question of: 'What is the name of that beautiful begonia? I must have one like that. Do give me the details. And what is this coffee? It's very much better than mine.'

Surprisingly, at lunch, Clarissa was much more forthcoming than of late. She volunteered at once that she and Anthony had been to see Winston in the hospital.

'How was he?'

'Very bad! I'd say, dying. He's gone a very pale waxen colour, no pink lips, and he can't remember anything except his early days. He couldn't remember that Heath had been to see him the day before about the Common Market, and he didn't seem to be listening when Anthony talked to him on the same subject. Yet, surprisingly enough, he does suddenly make sense. He had a little toy by his bedside — a grey square of wall with a black velvet cat crouching over it. I took the thing up and turned it so that the cat was looking the other way, and Winston, in the middle of the Common Market talk, turned and petulantly said, 'Why have you turned the cat the wrong way round?'

Clarissa talked about the recent sacking of almost the entire Cabinet, something that's not been done before. It was said that to save his face the Prime Minister wanted to give a 'new look' to the Cabinet. Politics, we all know, is a cruel business. I asked if Clarissa had heard the story of Macmillan having to go out and be sick between each sacking? 'Highly unlikely,' she said.

Clarissa described quite graphically this week's Garden Party at the Palace.

'But did you see anyone you know? I've never been invited, but I imagine it's a lot of those people you see all dressed up self-consciously standing very stiffly at the street corner as they wait hopelessly for a taxi.'

'Oh no, there's what they call "The Tent". There you see all the Ministers, and their wives, and the Corps Diplomatique and the ex-Prime Ministers, and it was very amusing to see Lord Eccles who just a few days beforehand would have said "I'll see you in The Tent", having to say, "I have to go over to tea with the hoi-polloi."'

It is strange to see the changes that have taken place in Clarissa's life since that day when she sat in my bedroom here at Broadchalke and wondered whether or not she should marry Eden. She'd been a bachelor girl a long time.

While he was Prime Minister the fiasco of Suez occurred. It was a bad time for them both. Anthony then became ill and from that moment Clarissa loved him as only a mother loves her child.

As a mother-nurse figure, Clarissa has acquired serenity of mind. She certainly has a *vie intérieure*. She can be by herself for a whole year on end, has a deep love of books, and of things of nature. There is no denying that she is a person of high taste and of first-class quality.

BROADCHALKE

August 10th

Perhaps success is merely superficial, but as I have always walked alone any that I have achieved has come entirely from my own machinations, or as a result of my own endeavours. I started out with very little talent, but a lot of strong ambition. This ambition has not abated with the years, and I have been fortunate. Maybe it was just as well that I was a late developer.

The ghastly fact that I am nearly sixty years old must be faced. With luck I may be able to carry on for some time making money, but equally I could soon find myself stranded and therefore bereft of confidence.

Cyril Connolly wrote that he was sorry for me; that I had worked so hard but that all my work was of an ephemeral kind. I feel this to be true, to the exaggerated extent that if I don't keep going with continuous new efforts I will be forgotten, even from one year to another.

August 11th

With the years I find my house in the country becomes ever more of a magnet. In fact I am always restless when away from it. Unlike rich people, I would never feel at ease leaving one house for another at set times of the year, or travelling for long periods on end before touching 'home' as in the game of 'Grandmother's steps'.

I want to stay put and watch a certain bud open. Even the three or four days in London are a great disturbance.

August 12th

The full day had started at eight o'clock this morning at Broadchalke when Mrs Talbot had, accompanied by the pug, brought in the tray, to be followed unexpectedly soon by the Sunday papers.

The newspaper headings were of the Russian astronauts circling the earth at 15,000 miles an hour, and busily telephoning and laughing as photographs of them and their voices were being relayed simultaneously back to the world below. The Russians intimate that they may send up five more astronauts before the end of the week and that this is a step towards making a landing stage in space from which a man can be propelled to the moon.

I always feel cheated and bypassed if I do not read all the Sunday papers in even a cursory manner. Today there were fascinating bits about the pale 'glamour' of the old days in an article wherein Robert Taylor blew the lid off MGM publicity. He described how 3,000 people had been cajoled into meeting him at a station and how two 'fans' had been paid by the office to hide under his sleeper.

Cyril Connolly's article on 'Rome' was a disappointment after his most brilliant and touching first article on the 'Grand Tour'. At last my 'Paris: Creators of Style' had appeared — a bit half-heartedly and disappointing after the amount of effort that had gone into it. It is a mistake to allow someone to alter one's immortal prose unless one follows through and agrees their interpretation.

I was delighted to skip through 'British Guiana' by my enemy, Evelyn Waugh, and to find it dull.

I did not feel particularly pleased, because I was conscious that this looked like being the end of the summer. The trees were autumnal. There was an air of *fin de saison*.

VISIT TO DENMARK

August

Eileen was there at Pelham Place, smiling and calm, to attend to all that was piled on my desk. She is indefatigable, impeccable and the fact that it was a Sunday afternoon and that she must cope with all these last-minute nonsenses in no way upset her. It took the two-and-a-half hours at our disposal to do all the packing, letters and photograph instructions, and it was only when the hired car was ready to take me to the airport that I suddenly faced up to the fact that I was going to Denmark.

'Here is your ticket and passport and this little map and book will show you where you're going. You see, there is Copenhagen; to get to Fyn you take the train east across country and you cross the sea and land at Nyborg.'

'And what money do they use? What are these you've given me?'

'Kroner — about twenty to the pound!'

It is Pauline (Baroness Philippe de Rothschild), the romantic self-styled 'lazy' woman, who, in her quiet, tactful way, has made this gaunt place into a living entity, and her own life into a nook of art.

It is fascinating to watch her. In fact I am never tired of doing so for she is like a chameleon, always changing, from beauty to ugliness and back again. As she sits and talks to you, leaning forward with the fluid grace of a dryad, you are hypnotised by her deep-set eyes, by their periwinkle blueness; you admire the modelling of the nose. As she speaks the mouth is beautiful, the arms and hands twist into peculiar shapes around her long body, and her streaming hair flies out in arabesques. She is Ondine, she is Garbo, she is a very young girl. Then she turns in profile and one is fascinated to see that beauty has entirely disappeared. She has a fish face, a fish mouth without form and positively no single chin. She is thick through the neck, and her shoulders are humped. One gasps when she comes in dressed for dinner wearing a short jet jacket and tight, white-satin trousers. Each evening she wears toreador satin trousers of different colours. When I was painting her she said: 'Of course with looks like mine one can't do anything except excuse oneself.' This was a rather tragic revelation of the truth; yet she does not accept the truth; she rises above it, and by determining to play the game, by wearing the most audacious St Laurent clothes, she succeeds in projecting a very personal and exotic brand of beauty.

Every gesture has been thought out; every pose compensates for some lack of symmetry in her frame, and the study has now developed into something that is of a 'second nature' to her. It is a brilliant feat, but then she is a clever woman, and to be admired for it.

Her face beams with pleasure when someone remarks upon a good action of a friend; she has heart and imagination to a rare degree, and although she has learnt how to appear at her best (placing head high, looking down her nose, pouting her lips, using the old tricks of *oeillade* to give further emphasis to her remarkable eyes), she emanates the refinement that is in her.

Pauline is, first and foremost, an intellectual. She reads without cease, has great knowledge of the classics and spends most of the time keeping up with the trends in modern literature. She is an authority on painting. She is extremely well versed in world affairs, in finance, and in politics, and she holds her own with her husband Philippe de Rothschild, who has a tireless curiosity for every subject. She pleases him with her remarkable flair for arranging the house with an individual elegance. A pot of flowers is never put in the centre of a table, always at the side. Objects are not placed symmetrically on the mantle-piece. It is typical of her that she should have chosen to bring him to this ravishing house in a remote part of Denmark; it reminds her of where she lived as a child. Without hope that it will ever be theirs, they have made plans to further beautify the house, which belongs to the Blixen-Finecke family.

At dinner one evening the talk was on the subject of coquettes who survived the 1914 war and until 1924 were about the last of their profession in our time. It was inspired by a discussion about the remarkable Jeanne Toussaint, the designer at Cartier, who is now the widow of the Baron Elie d'Orsel. Philippe had known her as a coquette when her name to intimates was Pom Pom. She was painted by Helleu. She had great taste and that is why Mizza Bricard admires her. She copies the way Pom Pom decorated her rooms in beige, her Greek and Louis XVI furniture and her method of stringing pearls together.

Said Philippe: 'It's a pity I didn't write about them, but I didn't know they'd ever be interesting. I was just having fun with them. For years I lived with Charlotte Bouquet; she was a remarkable woman. Her father kept a hotel in Toulouse and she had an ugly sister who lived with her in her apartment (very Jansen!) on the Quai d'Orsay. The sister was called

Blanche Bouquet, but it was smart to have English names at that time of the shingle and the short skirt, and to be rather masculine in appearance, so Charlotte Bouquet became Charlie Brighton. They weren't beautiful, these coquettes. They were clever and witty. They made you laugh and Charlie was like Mistinguette with a big mouth and too many teeth. But she had such style! She wore Chanel clothes, and none knew more about the way to please a man! Charlie always had the best men in Paris — always six-footers and very rich. I shared her with four others. Only once in five years did I ever run across any of the other men by mistake. It was beautifully managed. The morning was taken up with the dressmaker and the hairdresser. Then the afternoon was given up to her men.

'In the evening we always had the best table at the best restaurant. Charlie said that, when making an entrance, one must walk as straight as a die to one's seat, never looking to the left or to the right, or greeting anyone you knew. The *maître d'hôtel* had great respect for these women; they knew more about the men they were with than the men knew themselves, and they knew all the dealings in the banks and stockmarkets.

'Of course *coucheage* was always at the back of your mind, and that came later, but the coquettes were essentially amusing and their trump card was intimacy. They hardly ever gave parties, and when they did they were always flops. Honor Corbett, the last coquette in Paris, who could be so amusing, tried to give respectable parties but they were always terrible.'

I asked Philippe how it was arranged that you paid these ladies for their entertainment. 'Very easy. They just asked for a cheque. They said, "How do you expect me to live? Do you think I live on air? Who pays for my clothes, the apartment, the meals?" If you didn't pay enough they just tore up the cheque, and you'd have to think again. Thank heavens that never happened to me.

'And the interesting thing is that these women never became absorbed into society. They knew their place. They never wanted to be part of the world. They always remembered their beginnings; although Pom Pom eventually created a new and successful career for herself as Jeanne Toussaint, she would never invite Pauline to her apartment unless Pauline suggested that she should.'

KAREN BLIXEN AT RUNGSTED KYST

August 1962

I remembered that I had told Karen Blixen that I would get in touch with her again on my return from Fyn. I lifted the telephone receiver. After a moment I heard the familiar sepulchral voice.

'Oh, you're leaving so soon? Then can you come out and have *lunch* with me today?' 'I can't because my aeroplane leaves at four and I'd have to leave you by two o'clock.' 'Oh, I'm very sad about that. You said you'd come. Well you won't see me ever again, that's certain!' My heart stopped. I tried to remonstrate with her but she hung up. I knew I must rush to her immediately. Karen was a rare and wonderful woman whom I had admired for a long time. We were friends and I was proud of that. The last time we had met was in New York. She had appeared so ill and thin that I was convinced she would return to her native country to die.

No sooner had I arranged to have a hired car take me out to her house, three-quarters-of-an-hour away at Rungsted, than the telephone rang again. 'I wanted our conversation to end on a happier note.' 'I'm coming out to see you now. The car will be here in a few moments.' 'Well, you see, now you've arranged to go out to lunch with an old infirm woman.' 'But I'll be there before 11.30.' 'Oh well, that will be very nice. I am glad. We'll have a little drink together.'

I motored through the suburbs of Copenhagen on the way to Elsinore. At one small town I stopped to buy her some flowers. The florist was very sympathetic as he let me choose a flower here, and there, to make a bouquet of apricot and salmon pinks.

Karen was sitting in a large room on a white Biedermeier sofa against the sun, seemingly surrounded by white muslin curtains. She had an aura of extraordinary beauty. I wondered if tills was created by the colour of her pale, made-up face, lavender hair and blue sweater, or by the expression of the smiling, heavily blackened eyes. Her eyes have never appeared so shrunken, so small. She was even more wrinkled and thin than the last time I saw her — a gesticulating cadaver.

Karen welcomed me in her deep booming voice. 'Oh, I'm so glad to see you. It's so *good* of you to come.' She was delighted with the flowers.

'How young you look, Cecil! Come and talk. You see how thin I am. My arms are like sticks.' Only too readily she lifted the sleeve of her huge, thick jersey to reveal arms that were indeed matchsticks.

'I'm so weak, of course. I can't write. It's intolerable! The newspaper here wrote that I was now so thin that I'd got down to the cranium! I don't know if you would have liked to photograph my cranium?'

I was relieved to be asked just at that moment when the sun was coming so felicitously through the curtains. Her sweetly smiling face was sad, and the wrinkles looked like lacework. This woman who knows the whole of *King Lear* by heart carries the wisdom of the world in her eyes. 'You know I *can* walk if you'd like me to move to that other banquette.' I gave her a hand, and I could feel her elbow like a wishing bone. She smiled grotesquely. In some positions she looked like a scarecrow. But she was really beautiful, and I was excited to be given the chance to take such pictures.

'We must drink your health. Can you open that bottle of fizz?' I helped myself greedily to some excellent foie gras, and we were joined by the companion, kind, good, utterly devoted Miss Svenson, who had been with Karen for years. But the presence of this grey-haired, robust spinster somewhat prevented us from having a serious conversation. I thought the remark made by Karen on the telephone could be an opening to her views on meeting her saviour, and her regrets at quitting this life. Instead Miss Svenson recalled all the times we had met in New York.

'Do you remember when Mrs Selznick went to a lunch party by mistake? Mrs Paley said, "You've come on the wrong day," but Mrs Selznick didn't leave. And do you remember the time when we all went to Carson McCullers'?' Karen recalled the time when we had all stayed at Stratford, and had seen three Shakespeare plays in succession. She had not been too tired to go with Gielgud to see that lovely garden — Laurie Johnson's. But I had been exhausted by the intellectual effort and had hardly been able to concentrate on the last play.

We talked non-stop, and I did a sketch of her. But the time was passing.

'I must stand up to say goodbye to you.' I clasped her in my arms. The little bony body was nothing but a skeleton beneath the thick sweater and the grey flannel trousers. We kissed fondly and fervently; then I hurried out to the hired car. Karen came to the door to wave. Miss Svenson had tactfully disappeared so I had a last glimpse of this great person standing alone in the doorway, waving slowly and sadly. The chauffeur was proud to have seen this distinguished and well-known figure and he bowed low to her.

As we drove away from her she seemed to be peering into the distance. Her eyes became black holes in her face; a beautiful phantom that I shall always remember. I feel she cannot survive much longer. I hungrily looked my last, as the tiny figure turned to go out of my life for ever.

Part IX: African Journey

KENYA

January 1963

Sometimes the feathery trees and velvet mountains of Africa remind one of California; occasionally one thinks of Scotland or Ireland, and among the towering rhododendrons and maples one feels one is trespassing into some great prince's private parkland in India. Six thousand feet high above the sea, and walking along a forget-me-not bordered road leading to some very blue mountains one almost expects to hear yodelling, and one is surprised to see the natives are black, and are wearing sapphire beads and Tanagra-like draperies of terra-cotta.

The influence of African art on Picasso and most modern sculptors is evident. But one did not realise that Uccello would have delighted in the perspective of the jungle, and Pisanello, and others of the Italian Renaissance, in the detail of leaf and wild flower beneath the foot. Altdorfer could have delineated the elegant forests of saplings, and Velvet Brueghel the contrasts of smooth bark and rugged roots of banyan, the rich darkness of giant maple against the pale-grey blossom. Fragonard and all the eighteenth-century painters could have drawn inspiration from the leafy vistas; Courbet would have done justice to the juicy greenery, lowering crags and opulent waterfalls. The palette of Vuillard is ideal for the limpid greens and mauves of the life bordering the blue lakes.

VISIT TO A GAME RESERVE

It was not on a quest to kill, but to explore, and with the wish to admire, that we set forth from Nairobi to visit a game reserve. From that ugly, depersonalised new city, with its bougainvillea avenues, neon advertisements and junky Indian merchandising, we travelled back in distance many thousands of years.

The well-planned autoroute knifed its path through a wilderness of rock and dead trees where the ostrich will eat large stones to aid its gizzard and the stone-grey rhinoceros, that most prehistoric of king animals, will gobble thorn bushes with relish.

I was particularly fortunate to have Raymond Mortimer as a travelling companion on this safari. My friendship with him goes back to my earliest adult days. I remember the thrill of being invited by him to lunch in his Bloomsbury flat as soon as I left Cambridge. Throughout the years I have seen him from time to time and always found him delightful. He is marvellously well-informed and can see beauty in everything. Our journey was made even more enjoyable by our having Lettice Ashley Cooper with us. Lettice is extremely intelligent and perceptive. Perhaps her deafness has given her sharper intuitions, for although she may miss a great deal by not hearing the flow of strangers' conversations, she somehow gets to the pith of everything. She ruminates, and comes out with some very pointed and wise observations, about earth formations, the character of people or the habits of birds. Lettice knows a lot about the various races of the world and their religions. She is obviously well-educated and has read and remembered. She has a wry sense of humour, and is not embittered in any way.

Almost our first delight was to see a giraffe, eating at a convenient height a pepper tree. It looked as if it was made of dappled silk, pale primrose and honey-coloured. After exposing itself to our admiration, the giraffe, its head fluttering with white birds (the egrets, living off ticks and knowing where to find the most succulent), loped off in an absurd gangling dance.

Merely to stop the motorcar was to bring the Piero di Cosimo world close to us. At our feet a family of foxes; the young, so pretty with bat-ears and large eyes, were completely unabashed by our curiosity, while the parents skulked off to leave the young to their fate. But it was best not to leave for too long the sanctuary of the motor, and certainly not when a whole tribe of baboons swarmed onto the bonnet of the car.

It is almost inevitably dramatic to see one's first lion, for the 'King of Beasts' has received such inordinate publicity from Metro-Goldwyn and the British Empire. Already, at seven in the morning, after their breakfast kill, a lioness and her cubs had taken to the shade of the bush; nothing could be seen but the upstretched paw of the sleeping lioness. By dint of nosing our landrover into the sanctuary, within a few feet, we managed to disturb the sleepy animal who awoke, blinked at us with vague surprise, became bored with the attention of the camera, yawned, joined the rest of the family and continued her interrupted day's sleep.

The way to another pride of lions was signposted by the vultures waiting among the branches of a dead tree for the moment when the meal is abandoned and they can finish off the carcass of the recently-killed wildebeest.

The brutality of the jungle is epitomised by another scene of slaughter. Pools of blood, guts and the striped tail were all that remained of a zebra. A jackal, with the strongest teeth of all animals, was already running off with a large shinbone. A lion, with its dusty, over-life-size head, merely yawned at us, and we, in turn, were beginning to become bored with lions and to wonder if they should not remain in Trafalgar Square.

At Amboceli, still in Kenya, morning mists lifted to reveal Kilimanjaro, suspended above as if cut out of paper. A herd of buck gambolled past in the thick, dew-jewelled grass.

The animals rest or hide in the scrub while the sun is at its height. It is in the late afternoon, when shadows become mauve and the evening settles into itself, and everything seems at peace, that birds of prey, clean-cut and Egyptian-looking, swoop to the ground and perch on a rock. At this hour the lilac-breasted doves, rollers, magpies, blue and green chaffinches, weave through the aromatic scent of herbs and dark ferns. The late sun dapples the Arcadian glades, and suddenly a torrent of impala, pale biscuit-colour, appears. Eyes so brilliant-looking, ears cocked, listening; to our infinite delight they do not flee from sight, but remain nibbling at the long, thin grass. Only when we encroach too impetuously do they bound in athletic groups over fern and bracken to stand still again, staring.

The evening was fast closing in: a few eagles and hawks circled the periwinkle sky, but even the wart hog, whom Alan Moorehead flatters by calling it the 'Jolie Laide' of the desert, hurries off before it is too dark for even its safety.

Those other horrid scavengers among birds, long, obscene, pink-necked marabou storks, become panic-stricken at one's approach, and have a certain difficulty in becoming airborne.

On the way home to the safety of our camp, in the gloaming, we made our first acquaintance with the most dangerous of all wild creatures. Poised, or rather posed, on a white rock, surrounded by grey branches of a thorn tree, sat a young leopard. A twitch of his chest muscles, or a flick of the head, sends a chill down human spines. When the pale blue eyes are turned with curiosity onto oneself, terror and admiration are interwoven. White (only his back pale canary-yellow), with the blackest of velvet *tâches* placed in the most perfect Persian pattern, it is no wonder that he cannot, nor has any desire to, change his spots. With his beauty dots around the mouth, crisp white symmetry of whiskers, small neat oval of the twitching ears, the soft arms and paws, he is surely nature's masterpiece.

Raymond said: 'If I died during the night I should still feel it was worthwhile — one of the most wonderful days in my life.'

TANGANYIKA

In the misnamed 'Park' of Lake Manyara in Tanganyika we saw tropical forests with tall trees of every variety garlanded with parasitic fronds; and cascades of lilac and pale green blossom. In the viridian canopy above there were crickets to deafen one, and shrieking monkeys.

The sheaths and blades of tropical undergrowth gave way to a gently weaving procession: a herd of forty or fifty elephants appeared. How supple are their flapping butterfly ears as, weaving their trunks, with ivory tusks pointing, every heavy limb moves in graceful harmony. Elephants seem less like themselves than their counterfeiters in the pantomime. One cannot believe that those baggy trousers do not contain well-trained performers!

But although the elephant appears to have small, unseeing eyes and moves in slow rhythm, he is quick to escape out of range: perhaps fortunately — for if he had a mind to it, only one of the herd could, within seconds, reduce our landrover to a mere sardine tin.

On the way to the great crater of Ngoro Ngoro we passed mountains like the backsides of green elephants; the dark-red earth ditches abounded in black and gold snakes and giant flowers. Masai shepherds and warriors with elaborate hair plaits and earth-red draperies, bring home their flocks to share their mud dwellings.

At a height of eight-thousand feet we looked down upon the crater — bean-shoot green plains surrounded by a cerulean wall of mountain. It is one of the great sights of the world. It was an opportunity to see the earth as it was at the time of the Creation. The impression was so overwhelming that one became speechless.

The descent into the crater took us down winding crags that are filled with every sort of rare plant, shrub and flower. Trees are taller, grass is longer, and forget-me-nots are bluer. In the crater are forests, plains, lakes. On the edge of a large sheet of water fringed with poison green rushes, continuous bird ballet is performed. The long islands of pale pink are flamingos, and the paler ones, cranes. They walk or paddle by the water's edge in a long crocodile procession.

A group of water buffalo, caked with pale grey mud, with pinprick, blinking eyes, wide decorative horns and low ears, remind one of early Chinese sculpture.

Even as we looked in awe and marvel, darkness enveloped the neighbouring mountains and the skies became menacing yellow and grey. Our log cabins, complete with lamp and wood fire, welcomed us. Raymond quoted: 'We have sipped the milk of Paradise.'

MADAGASCAR

The first glimpse of this island was promising — pale rice-shoots in the paddy fields, energetic, muscular women working in the muddy water, eucalyptus trees, frangipani, red earth, villages with tall, coloured houses. In fact, even the humblest shack had elegant proportions, wooden balustraded balconies, and some are painted as if by children in bright chalk colours. A special light gave uniformity and grace, and pleased the aesthetic sense.

The people in the streets seemed to be a mixture of races — Chinese, Indian, Arab and African. Women and men wore white draped shawls, and the men an assortment of fantastic European hats — highwayman-esque or Robin Hood-ed.

Madagascar is the third largest island in the world. Marco Polo gave it its name. King Radama was the first king. He encouraged Europisation and, under the influence of an Irish soldier in the Indian Service, Sergeant James Hastie, learned to sleep in a bed, take a bath, play cards and listen to the striking of clocks, before he met an early death in 1828 at the age of thirty-five. Unfortunately he was succeeded by Queen Ranavalona the Terrible, who is said to have been responsible for over two hundred thousand men and women being put to death in the most ghastly ordeal of poison, mutilation, and stoning. At her coronation in 1868 idols were burned and Protestantism became the state religion. Queen Victoria sent the Malay Queen a huge bible and an album of coloured family photographs. But, after a certain amount of misunderstanding and trickery in 1895, Madagascar joined the French Empire and Queen Ranavalona III sadly went into exile in Algeria, where she died in 1917. Today Madagascar is a Republic with the President living on the hilltop in a large castle.

Tananarive, the capital city, is a tightly-packed cluster of heterogeneous buildings covering the mountain top and glistening in the crystal sunlight. We discovered every sort of architectural style: Chinese, *art nouveau* and 1890 Louis XVI cheek by jowl, and we were reminded of San Francisco, Singapore and Karachi.

Dominating the entire city is the four-square Queen's Palace built in the medieval style. This was originally made of wood, but, in order that it should become suitably grandiose, the Scottish architect Cameron covered it with stone. It is flanked by enormous wooden, thatch-roofed chalets that are either tombs, temples, or palaces of former rulers.

Queen Ranavalona II, who was an enthusiastic pen friend of Queen Victoria, whom she addressed as 'Ma chere soeur', lived in a charming Chelsea-ish house with small-paned, deep-set sash windows. The Balmoral influence can be seen in stag-decorated inkstands and chairs, gold-embossed flock paper from London, red-velvet ottoman, inlaid floors, gilt-framed portraits and huge coloured photograph-portraits. Even the garden is a paradox of exotics with formal borders of marguerites and salvias; and the scarlet-hatted brass bandsmen practising under an enormous avenue of royal figtrees play the same selections we hear on the front at Eastbourne.

Victoria's influence can also be seen in the black Queen's choice of jewels which, though of no rare stones, are in imitation of the coral coronets and sapphire and gold diadems seen in Winterhalter portraits.

The Queen's throne room has an Alice in Wonderland quality with the crimson velvet canopy over gilt throne, Victorian chandeliers and clocks under glass, for with the silk on the walls looking like the shabby guest bedroom of a large house in the Lake district the pretence at grandeur fails poignantly, but the attempt has great charm.

My particular treat was to see the Court clothes, all made for the Queen in Paris by Lemoine. They were in the bustle style in bright scarlets or orange and heavily embroidered almost all over in design of jasmine or wheat ears, and some of the pants were slashed like those worn by Elizabethan courtiers; and there were many small Empire-style bodices that were an inspiration, for they were made of most unexpected material — moss green tufted velvet, or cabbage-rose patterned wool cretonne, and the skirts of scarlet or yellow had embroidered hems that were works of art.

Nothing was more rewarding than the visit to the market (Rova). It took place in the square. Large white umbrellas covered each stall and the sunlight and shadow playing on these geometric shapes created bizarre abstract patterns. The reflected light under the umbrellas flattered the serried rows of sugar-cane sticks, the soft mounds of tomatoes and the opalescent pyramids of eggs; the mountains of pineapples, plums and bananas were like Braque 'still-lives', and the spikes of black bullrushes, the billowing bundles of carnations, the clouds of roses, the zinnias and the tuberoses were dazzling.

But it was the rainy season and in the late afternoon with the first heavy drops this impermanent city of white umbrellas broke up in a trice. The people, in their bright-coloured cottons, packed their wares, climbed on carts and wagons and left behind a deserted sea of refuse.

Madagascar is the home of the gentle lemur, birds of brilliant plumage, and many varieties of chameleons. Mountains rise in some places to over ten thousand feet; I saw hot springs, extinct volcanoes and forests like tapestries; rare ferns, orchids,

233

and waterfalls; this vanilla-scented island is indeed a tropical paradise.

PARIS: PRINCE FELIX YOUSSOPOFF

In Paris I had a rendezvous that delighted me, a visit to the past, to Prince Felix Youssopoff, the beautiful, royal, dignified homosexual who murdered Rasputin. I have tried hard to get in touch with this remote figure each time I've come to Paris. This time my contacts, Tony Gandarillas and Prince Paul, were of no help, so I telephoned him myself and asked if I could come and see him. He seemed baffled. What did I want? I told him and he said he did not want to be photographed, but yes I could come and talk to him. I had trouble in finding the street and the house. When I rang at an orange-red painted gate there was no reply. Parents waiting for their children to come out of a school watched with curiosity while I rang in vain. At last the door was opened by the Prince, very sprightly in spite of his seventy-nine years, a tall figure in blue serge, like a cavalry officer or ski instructor.

We sat in a small, dark sitting room full of ikons, *démodé* photographs and huge Czarist portraits. He spoke in a deep Russian voice, very *racé*, with innate dignity. He is almost blind but his eyes are still beautiful and deep-lidded and had been liberally made-up with dark pencil. He talked of mutual friends: Diana Cooper, Marjorie Anglesey; but he seemed preoccupied and disinterested in the Paris of today that I know. Rather he was involved in helping people who are nervously upset or even a bit mad. He says that often nervous troubles are alleviated by being aired to strangers. He is mixed up in all sorts of religious, mystical, occult ideas and showed me a whole series of paintings of fantastic heads that he had done in ink and water-colour. He had never painted before, and once he had done these heads and put them away in a cupboard the talent had left him.

I'm told he is very stingy, but does have money. Today he was worried that the pipes in the house in the country had burst and he would have to pay for a whole new heating system. His Russian housekeeper appeared with wine and biscuits which we ate in this awful little dining room. The bedroom was a charming room with tall windows letting in a lot of light. There were many mementoes of the past; portraits in pastel and oil, etchings, and photographs. The furniture was cream-coloured and the huge cane-work imitation Louis XIV bed had belonged to Grand Duchess Dagmar; the enormous dressing-table with a three-fold mirror was covered with a vast array of bottles, and make-up pencils of every colour.

A certain resistance to being photographed was soon worn down and the old boy posed with extreme dignity. There was nothing ludicrous about him and he defied one's amusement. It was amazing to see this gaunt, birdlike man, whose sculpted head appeared on the chimney-piece, and on bookshelves, and who was photographed in Imperial pearls, now sitting in this microcosm of another age and another world.

He did not seem to have any regrets. His wife was in bed, ill of a cold. He seems to get along well with her, but is said to be ungenerous with their daughter who now has a debutante to launch.

It would have been an even more interesting morning if I had dared broach the subject of the Rasputin murder, but I was already late for lunch with Lilian so that topic must wait until the next time.

Part X: Return to Hollywood, 1963

HOLLYWOOD REVISITED

February 19th

I was going to Hollywood to work on the film of *My Fair Lady*. But could I really be going away for one whole year? Would there be no glimpse of England in summer? Would I miss my garden?

Not that London, or the country, had been particularly pleasant during the last two months. In fact ever since the return from East Africa the snow, ice and Alaskan cold had made travel even between Salisbury and London somewhat difficult.

The work at Covent Garden designing *Turandot* and Freddie Ashton's new ballet, *Marguerite et Armand*, had been arduous. The strain had been intense, and my physical condition was weakened by a long bout of colitis.

Thirty-five years ago I could think of nothing more wonderful than going to Hollywood to work on designing a great film. But Hollywood has changed and so have I.

Eleven hours after flying over ice floes, icebergs, snow-capped, jagged mountains, a white frozen world from which one would never be saved if forced to make a landing, the jet plane landed in a mist in an unrecognisably enlarged Los Angeles airfield. We were ahead of schedule, by one hour, so the great Irving Lazar was not there to meet me, but a nice note of welcome and flowers from various friends greeted me at the hotel.

Memories floated back of my first visit here when Hollywood was all Spanish. Anita Loos, Gloria Swanson and the Fairbanks were reigning; memories of Ina Claire, and photograph sessions for *Vanity Fair*. How thrilled I had been to be allowed inside a studio; to pass the police at the door was like entering the pearly gates. I remembered the time we rehearsed and played *Lady Windermere* here, and most poignant of all were the memories of Greta, of the days when I did not know her, when I met her, and the last time she lived here, and here was her house from which I used to walk back, very tired, late at night, hardly able to manage the steep incline of the drive to the Beverly Hills Hotel.

Irving Lazar, my brilliant agent, came to my room to give me a few pointers: I'd go on the payroll tomorrow. I'd better find a little house of some sort as I was going to be here a considerable time. Irving, a mole-sized giant, fives in a vast luxurious apartment-block; he has a large collection of modern pictures, including a Picasso; the dollar bills roll in and roll out, and his car was, of course, a marvellous *café-au-lait* and black Rolls.

We went to a charming house for dinner. By the time the evening was over it was according to English time seven-thirty in the morning. Little wonder that the evening had gone by in somewhat of a haze. But the bright talk, about films, had seemed amusing and a new Hollywood was already unfolding itself to me.

February 24th

An evening with Christopher Isherwood and Don Bacardy at their house by the sea was an utter delight. Christopher biting and munching his lips, blinking his eyes, and sitting in a blue window, talked with such wealth of interest. Stravinsky was suddenly stricken and couldn't come, which was a minor disaster, but his wife Vera and Bob Craft contributed to a most sympathetic and charmingly civilised evening.

Vera Stravinsky had been the Queen in *Sleeping Beauty* and kept laughing about her age. 'I'm not going to tell you how old I am.' She is a lesson in how to compensate for lost youth and beauty. She is now fat, and a mess, but she has style which does not make one regret anything. She has acquired a robust magnanimity towards the world. She has the common touch, and knows how to remain pure in this most drossy of worlds. Madame Stravinsky, a Scandinavian who is more Russian than the natives of Russia, was at her best from the moment that she entered the house and started reminiscing about Diaghileff. He was such a dandy, but because he was hopeless about money and keeping up his wardrobe, his underclothes were found to be full of holes when he died. He was a wonderful impresario; he was susceptible to energetic youth. All the boys suffered when he died; one of them went so far as to polish the nails of the dead man.

It is interesting to note how the Stravinskys, Christopher, Aldous Huxley and Gerald Heard are hardly conscious, in their own little world out here, of the vulgarity around them.

March

This evening was a real change. The Brodys were giving a party for the French Ambassador and his wife and Mary Lasker, and the Wrightsmans had arranged for me to be asked. The Brodys live in a large modern house filled with contemporary pictures and sculpture. It is everything a modern house should be, with ceilings open to the skies, large plate-glass walls, gardens filled with Rodin, Giacometti and Maillot; and indoors, great trees growing. The effect of tropical green leaves against Picassos is exciting. One wall was taken up by a vast Matisse ceramic. Seventy people sat at tables decorated with red rose umbrellas. An enormous number of magnums were drunk and the French Ambassador in a speech complimented the host on the excellence of Californian wines. People have given millions, and collected more millions, to make Los Angeles a worthy place. Up until now people living here have not had much civic sense, perhaps because they felt they had no roots here. But now it is different. California has developed enormously, and with its electronics, motors, oil and nuclear experiments is one of the most important states in the country, and Los Angeles is its principal city.

Dinner with Merle Oberon

Irving and Ellin Berlin were fellow guests at Merle Oberon's dinner party. Irving is amazingly young for seventy-five. He has the grand manner combined with the personality of a little boy. He told about song hits that weren't recognised at first, about Ethel Levey, George M. Cohen, Fanny Brice, the Dolly sisters and Charles Dingham. He reminisced about Gaby Deslys, 'plump but a star'; she said 'crapped' up the stairs instead of crept.

Ellin was relaxed but tough. Irving said, 'You're very bitchy tonight. Friends will wonder how I stayed married to you all these years.' Merle was at her very best; relaxed, calm, no hostess's giggles or wild eyes. She looked beautiful in a Japanese kimono; only the house was awry, but that can't be mentioned. The sympathetic, cosy and interesting evening had another merit — it was over by ten o'clock.

A NEW FRIEND

March 24th

I went to San Francisco for the weekend and there I met Kin Hoitsma, a tall Scandinavian boy who struck me as being particularly sensitive and gentle. He had the most sweet smile. Eventually we talked with one another. I discovered by baffling degrees that he was an art historian, working for his degree and studying and lecturing at Berkeley University.

His apartment had dried grasses on the window-sill and eight daffodils were very charming in a black pot. There was everywhere evidence of little money, but pure taste. He had cut up a book of Picasso drawings to hang on the walls of his lavatory.

Kin turned out to be someone of the utmost simplicity and honesty and intellectual integrity. He presented a tremendous challenge, and although essentially a difficult character, solitary and deep thinking, he inspired me to the sort of gentle emotion that I have not felt for a long time.

San Francisco: April

I went to Stockton Street to see Kin. On second acquaintance I liked him more. He is subtle; he never says too much, although he can be talkative, as indeed he was when I arrived and watched him blacking and polishing his enormous shoes. He likes Blake and anything mystical, some of Monet's paintings, some Grecos and Renoir. He adores Mozart, 'who makes a tragedy of frivolity', and plays his music throughout his rooms.

He becomes a real professional when, with Grunewald curling fingers, he turns the pages of his book on Masaccio and the great Donatello. He showed me pictures of late Botticellis which are not so well-known as the more generally popular, early ones. They are violent in form, line and colour and are wild.

It was with intense pleasure that I listened to and learnt from my new friend. He gabbles, as if with a marble in his mouth and another in his throat, about his pet subjects, and one is caught up in his boyish enthusiasm. Kin has great physical strength. He is an enthusiastic games player and once represented his country in fencing.

This new friendship is something I am deeply grateful for; it is rare and profoundly satisfying and compensates for much that I have had to put up with since leaving home.

Kin had had for dinner last night a loaf of brown bread, cottage-cheese and fruit.

May 3rd

Talk never ceased for a moment throughout dinner and all the way back to San Francisco. We had travelled 300 miles since starting off this morning. We talked about sex, marriage, Los Angeles, the difficulties of adolescence, the climate of San Francisco (cultural and physical), about flowers. Kin likes dopey white chrysanthemums and a few simple yellow flowers; he likes green plants and he dislikes more things than he likes. Kin's taste is very strong and primitive and impressive on all counts. We were both utterly worn out when we got back to the favoured, well-known privacy of Stockton Street.

Friday

The evening at Diana Vreeland's was a joy. Diana's new wig-like hairdo was unbecoming. But her important responsibilities as Editor-in-Chief of *Vogue* do not seem to have got her down in the least. In fact she was soaring higher in more fantastic upward spirals than before. Truman brilliantly related his latest experiences with the two murderers he had been to see in 'Death Row'.

Truman is quite changed in appearance. No longer is he the elfin waif; he has become a solid man of parts. It has always amazed me how much at home he is in the world, able to talk with anyone on his own terms, with no reserves or apologies. He told us how he had come to possess the grimmest document that one could imagine. As his horrifying saga unfolded, he unconsciously revealed the magnitude of his development as a story-teller, the wealth of his experience and the strength of his imagination.

In the terrible prison Truman had not been able to summon up the courage to ask Perry if he could be present at his hanging. He felt that although Dick was not as good a friend, he could ask him. He produced his fountain pen; Dick wrote the appalling sentence, then put the pen in his sock and refused to give it back. Dick then started to taunt Truman. 'I've never liked you. Perry was your friend and I've hated you for the five years you've been around and if I give you your pen it will be through your heart.' 'What good would that do you?' 'Justification! Do you realise that before you could call the guard, with that pen I could put out both your eyes?' 'And what good would that do?' 'Satisfaction!' By showing no sign of panic, by telling Dick that it would not help his last appeal, Truman proved his supremacy and Dick threw back the pen at him. 'I Dick … hereby in respect of $250 being paid to my mother, appoint Truman Capote to be my official witness at my hanging.'

Truman asked us, 'Do you think I was justified in getting that permission from him for such a small amount of money?' He had explained that a well-known lawyer had said it would be impossible for him to be present at the hanging as the leading magistrate did not like him.

Truman also told of other murderers he had come across in this prison — two very beautiful young men who had gone through five states murdering for kicks as they went; both strangling respectable housewives with bull whips while performing the sexual act.

EDIE'S DINNER

June

After dinner at Edie Goetz's, Fellini's 8½ was shown. I did not understand one word of it, since there were no subtitles and the plot is not indicated. Nevertheless, I am not at all 'literal-minded' and seldom pay any attention to the mechanics of a plot, and I found this film visually rhythmic. It was like a wonderful ballet, with extraordinary types, and such daring wit that it was never one moment too long. Billy Wilder has the usual Hollywood complex about hating anything non-commercial. 'It's such impertinence indulging his esoteric, snobbish pretensions. It's an insult to the public.' Edie did not like it much.

Hitchcock, whom I've always loathed, was a fellow guest and said to David Selznick (apropos of the Profumo case) that it had cut England down to size. The English were so arrogant — didn't this serve them right? Didn't I think the British were arrogant? Without knowing why, I have been gunning for Hitchcock for many years. There is nothing more unattractive than a man decrying his own country in another one. He did not know what had hit him when I burst out at him, 'Of course the English are arrogant, and with good reason! I love them for it. I love arrogance!'

Hitchcock said that films should be made to give pleasure to people who weren't interested in films as an art form. 'The films are not an art form. It's selfish of people who make films for their own pleasure and interest.'

Then we started to fight about artists in films — like Fellini. Hitchcock brought the subject round to himself. He said he was the father of the avant-garde in France; that all these young people were doing very badly. They all called on him for help. 'I hope you give them money,' I remarked.

'That's very rude,' said Mrs Goldwyn on my right.

'Aren't fathers there to do just that?' I answered. The evening was nightmarish, but good to laugh about afterwards.

NUREYEV

June 27th

The evening was interesting in that it was spent at a party given for Rudi Nureyev. I never know in what mood he is going to be and was quite expecting him to be cold and disdainful. But, no, he was slightly drunk and very coy. I made a great play of flattery and he fell for it with every dimple in his thin cheeks. We hugged and kissed and displayed a great love for one another and I proposed that he should come and live with me. It was all very agreeable and an amusing comedy. But in between the lines he threw me a few home truths. People have been very mean with him; he will continue with them, but they must pay him. He will do TV work here in New York, but the US Government takes all in taxes. I felt sorry for him. He is, for all his fame, a lone wolf.

The party was one of Hollywood's most select but, like all Hollywood parties, it had no homogeneity, no atmosphere, and an awkward wait before any food was served.

On my way out I went to find Nureyev in his bedroom. 'Rudi? Rudi?' I found him sitting in his great bedroom dangling a loose shoe. 'What are you doing here? Are you sad?'

'Yes, and very lonely — this awful house — you suffer so. Maybe I have five days in Paris with my friend, but we have been travelling a month without meeting; and when you love you are apt to be sad and there's no hope for us. We can't work together. It is *always* travelling for me; always on the road — without a window.'

'You see ballet people are so silly. They do as they're told. They never think. Nobody understands me, perhaps Margot a little from time to time, and Freddy's nice, but he offers me nothing, and they hate me. But I don't care.'

I tried to cajole him, to make jokes; I told him of the beauties of being in love if one did not suffer too much; and how lucky when it happened painlessly. But Rudi is a Russian and I don't expect he loves painlessly. He came out to the car. 'Would you like to go for a ride with me?'

'No, I must stay here. The others will be arriving from the ballet.'

June 29th

The ballet (*Giselle*) was badly lit, terrible *décor* and costume. But the evening was lifted to greatness and poetry by Nureyev. He seemed to have become even more at home in the first act of this old barnstormer and smiled and reacted with genuine simplicity; but in the second tragic act the 'bigness' of his pride, his arrogance, was something we don't see in the theatre nowadays. I was transported. The Los Angeles audience, who

245

were really knowledgeable and appreciated the difficulty of every feat, applauded ecstatically.

It was a revelation to discover how wide the appeal of ballet has become. Although the setting was frowzy, and the theatre hideous and unworthy (one could hardly hear the orchestra), the quality of genius gave the evening excitement that is unforgettable. Margot was superb.

July 3rd

My feelings about the ballet *Marguerite and Armand*, on which I had worked so hard, were mixed. The auditorium dwarfed the set, the curtain did not stretch to the sides and the lighting was very rough. The orchestra played an introduction with chiming bells that I thought poor in quality, but once the ballet started I was carried along in a transport of emotion. It is a remarkable work despite what the critics said. It is packed with drama and one sits tingling, on edge in case one misses a nuance.

I was very pleased with my contribution and considered that it hit exactly the right note. The ballet conveyed, in fact, just the atmosphere that we had hoped that it should. Margot's performance is her best and she shows herself to be another Duse. The taste she displays is amazing and she is made a beauty through the quality of her spirit. Nureyev, too, is the quintessence of all romantic passion; smiling in the early scenes and like a tragic clown (even to the red nose and pale eyes) at the last. Fred Ashton's work is inspired, and it is everything that I like in ballet.

It was a thrill to see that the result of our labours had turned out as we had hoped. The audience screamed. But it was good to hear George Cukor yelling himself hoarse. He said, 'I never remember shouting in a theatre before, and the thought is painful for me, but your work is beautiful!' My mind was in a state of elation. This should have been a happy evening.

AUDREY'S TRIAL

July 11th
Audrey Hepburn's Ascot hat was tried on. She looked incongruous under this enormous confection of lace, striped ribbon, ostrich feathers, lilac, wheat and rosebuds, wearing a print dress, ballet shoes and with her Yorkshire terrier on her lap.

This week has been music week; and tomorrow Audrey does her flower girl in a separate cubicle while the orchestra plays outside under Previn's baton; it is an ordeal, but if her voice is not up to standard, Audrey will be the first to admit it. She will have done her best. No one worked harder than she, and the improvement in her voice is extraordinary.

Audrey has a marvellous wish to be as authentic as possible, and not to cheat in the way most stars would. Her face is wide and her head flat; by building the *coiffures* wider we have made her head look flatter. She is willing to be as ugly as anyone wishes in the early sequences, but she feels that when the time comes, she should be allowed to be beautiful.

July 25th
'They're testing the Covent Garden set with the rain machine and there are some men and women lined up for you on 9.' The women were appalling, not beautiful Hollywood showgirls as I'd hoped.

Buck was rattled when I said they wouldn't do. It seems a question of money is involved, but really beautiful girls are expensive and, in a film costing millions, I should have thought an acceptable charge. As for the set, it was an enchantment, a Gustave Doré of London to the life. The tall proportions of the buildings, with the personages small in scale in comparison, are very satisfactory. The signs, the gas lamps and every detail of this sort are extraordinarily exact.

I was almost in tears (of nostalgia) when the rainstorm fell and the place was flooded. I almost felt I was back in London — a very beautiful beginning to any story.

This is the beginning of the end of a very happy phase of this picture. My experience in the wardrobe has been inspiring, exciting and easy-going. It is never anything but a pleasure to work there, even when difficulties have to be overcome.

Then the delightful event of Kin arriving from San Francisco. I met him at the airport, and played hookey all afternoon, deciding on the spur of the moment to go to Forest Lawn. This extraordinary piece of commercialism has to be seen to be believed. We gasped at the Last Supper being recreated for posterity. We saw the mausoleum with the names of all the dead on marble slabs with torpedo vases placed ready for flowers. We saw the museum and the souvenir shop. We laughed secretly at the appalling bad taste and the hidden music. I realised that this was for real.

ALBUQUERQUE

July 27th

Early start in smog. Los Angeles in a peasouper and the freeway to Santa Anna so ugly, but by being courageous Kin and I were rewarded. At last we came out into citrus groves and sunshine, and in spite of bad traffic on the holiday roads arrived in San Diego in time to take the ferry for Coronado. Lunch at the huge white modern hotel in a huge brown wooden dining room. The clientele, somewhat understandably, very respectable older people. Thence to the Zoo. The flamingos, brilliant pink-orange, the first delight and wonder. Real enthusiasm here, followed by such joys as the patterned snakes (thousands of years ago they were being made in 1920 futuristic designs!) and the birds are always my delight — cockatoos, brilliant parrots, ibis, osprey; but this time we were thrilled by the 'walk-through' aviary. Here the cage is so large that birds can fly into the tallest trees; they have space to lead their lives unconcerned by the gaping hordes who pass through to wonder at the doves and Chinese pheasants, or the ducks getting splashed at the waterfalls. There were lemurs to remind one of Madagascar, and tapirs to remind one of André Previn.

The iguanas were a special treat, some silvery and orange, as if they were out of *Midsummer Night's Dream*. I envied the seals their swimming fun.

We drove on to the border of Mexico. A hundred yards over the line at Tiahuana all was dirty, rundown and vulgar. We were appalled by the poverty of the country, the scenery grey and arid, the people living in broken-down tin shelters and altered buses. We drove till late evening to arrive at Encenada, and looked in vain for a hotel. All motels advertised 'no vacancy'. We found one disused hotel and garden quite attractive but barbed wire across the door. Where to go? We continued along the coast in the gloaming to a motel and camping site. Here was a city of trailers situated on some mud flats. Never have I seen anything so awful, so depressing; yet here too we were unwelcome — no vacancy. We returned to Encenada and went to a horrible-looking Spanish motel that we had scorned before. With what relief we were told we were lucky — one room left.

Tourist attractions galore and a cabaret of incredible ineptitude at the Balia where we dined (carefully!). Thence to visit the tourist junk shops where a *Venus de Milo*, sadly squat, was painted bright shiny black. Mexican peons in plaster squatted asleep under large hats. Hideous! Hideous! Nothing to do but laugh, and in each other's company we laughed.

After our night of sightseeing (a dreary strip joint), we were set upon by the local tarts. We returned to our beds but not long after losing consciousness we were treated to a Tennessee Williams drama of the utmost squalor and fascination. In the next-door room a man and wife carried out at full volume a tremendous row.

The husband had been out whoring. 'When I married you I didn't think you'd do this to me.' 'Now you know!' 'My best friend said you were a lousy son of a bitch, but I loved you. How I hope you die and hope you'll suffer for all you've done.' The woman taunted the man more and more, calling him names and defying him to hit her. The language used was vile and horrid and the taunts were fulfilled. 'Go on, throw that thing at me. You've done it before and I had to have twenty-seven stitches put in. Do it again, I'm not afraid.' Eventually the glass bottle was dropped crashing to the ground. Soon the blows fell, the woman screamed. 'Help! Help!' The fat proprietress of the motel rushed out and yelled: 'You bum, you lay off.' The wife continued to scream. Any moment the woman could have been murdered, but no one stirred. The last thing the proprietress wanted was to call the police. None of us would get mixed up, for that would have meant going to jail and God knows what protection we would have had. That is a terrible feeling and one that makes one shudder and long for the safety of honesty.

Suddenly the wife ran out of the room chased by her husband, and got into her car. She backed it; crashed into another; drove off and into another car. She paid no heed to the shouts of 'Hold it! Hold it!' from the neighbours who had not moved to help her from being murdered, but were on the spot when it came to a question of damage to their cars. The proprietress took up her role of admonishment with resumed force. 'You lousy son of a bitch, treating this place as if it were a no-good brothel.'

BACK TO FILMING

August 3rd

The week started well with an early fitting of Audrey wearing her dress for the last scene. It is important that this strikes the right mood of romantic individualism. It is a pale pastel-mauve muslin confection and Barbara has made it to look as if it had no seams. It is like a froth built on Audrey.

It is the custom of theatre and film people to swoon at the sight of anything that is newly made. Joe Hyatt is a big, rugged man, and he telephoned to say he had been hanging around just to see Audrey in the dress which had been on the stand on Friday afternoon and he had gazed at it for fifteen minutes. He said it was a 'Poom', and he cracked, 'Yer know I'm generally taken only by how much a dress costs — this time I'm hypnotised by the dress itself. It's great!'

August 9th

Vignettes were taken showing the 'grand life' leaving the opera hurrying past the desolated Covent Garden market. The rain was pouring through the arc-lights onto a hackney carriage drawn by a black, shiny, wet horse which descended a ramp, slipping and falling with the carriage on top of it. No time to bother about slipped horses! In the distance I saw some of the women in the waterproof capes, and to my horror saw their heads were twice the size they should be. George Cukor said this would not show in the distance as the figures were so small in this shot, and that in the next one the crepe hair covering their coiffures could be removed; this was just to prevent the ladies' heads getting soaked. My spirits were dampened also at the many incorrect sights. But then my fever was raging. I felt red hot, my throat was very sore. I was suddenly stricken with this bug that has lowered my resistance for five days now.

Their taste pitted against mine. And there were unforeseen disappointments. Where's that nice honey-blonde girl who wore the red foxes? Oh, we lost her and Miss Smith, she couldn't get her work permit. Good girls lost and horrors found.

August 19th

It was a beautiful day; so Kin and I motored to a small village near Sansaleto which I believe is called Tiburan. Here on a quayside with bobbing boats and white houses among the pines, high on the overlooking hillside, we had lunch. With the sunshine and gulls it was like any boat resort, particularly like the Isle of Wight, and I felt pleased with life.

Kin is really incredibly well informed on aspects of art history. He showed me how precise an instrument his mind is when he translated, with the help of a dictionary, a German paragraph by an art philosopher. He not only understood but memorised the passage which, doltish as I am, still baffled me when re-repeated. It was to do with the artist being an idiot if he ignored nature in his interpretation, but a mere copy of nature was of no interest.

Isobel Elsom had to be rigged out in a new costume. She pined for the spangles and the Greek band and was sad at having to look her own period.

Suddenly Jeremy Brett appeared from London bringing with him a whiff of home in the form of a package of my hair lotion from Eileen.

August 23rd

Hangman's call. The Freeway successfully negotiated; already life going on in a big way at the studio. Coffee canteens very popular and a scene of enormous activity in the make-up department with rows of women being coiffed as grand ladies or cockneys.

Audrey appeared. 'I was so excited I couldn't sleep all night.' The British Consul and about fifty photographers were signs of the great occasion.

August 25th

My only engagement was to go to dinner at Audrey's for Mel Ferrer's birthday party. Managed to find a pretty watercolour sketch of spring flowers to give him and went off in great spirits to enjoy myself. The party showed the best sides of everybody I met. They take their 'private' life very seriously and separately from their careers. This was a family party, only close friends. Their buddies included Cathleen Nesbitt, the Yul Brynner's and Rupert Allen.

At a given moment during the dinner (served at a table down by the pool) there came across the lawns a torchlight procession of Shaun (2½), carrying a candlelit birthday cake, accompanied by Audrey and Mel's children.

Audrey looked very gauche and plain, with huge flat feet and yet just as appealing as when she is a beauty. Talked to Yul about the loss of Gertie Lawrence and he told me that Rodgers and Hammerstein had been beastly to work for; that, after appearing for them for four years in *The King and I*, he never even received a word of thanks after the final performance; and that they'd tried to get rid of Gertie Lawrence. There is a clause in the contracts that if stars are ill for three weeks the management can give them notice. On the day that Gertie died they sent a letter demanding her resignation.

August 26th

Christopher Isherwood's birthday party given by Bill and Paul, Dru. Gavin Lambert, Jim and Jack, and Gore Vidal — an amusing evening, excellent talk, the company eating sprawled on divans and on the floor. Hilarious and witty talk about Cole Porter burning himself and likening him to those Buddhist monks who commit suicide. Discussion of Mary Macarthy's new book. Gore really very entertaining; success seems to have sweetened him.

September 1st

We talked about Alan Lerner's possible project on Chanel; I had never realised how much time he had spent closeted with this lady talking about her life. She had been very frank, and disarming up to a point, but he said, 'Now come off it — tell me what your life has really been like.' It appeared she was most ashamed of her early poverty.

September 7th

Breakfast for Kin had been a drink of river water and some raisins. I had a few raisins but thought coffee would help. It took a lot of trouble on Kin's part to boil the water. But he loves all these jobs and it is wonderful to watch him moving among the rocks with such grace. After the rites of washing and shaving in these conditions, we went on to another part of the forest to sit and muse and then I watched Kin fishing.

When Kin talks of everyday things, such as changing his clothes or washing, instead of quoting contemporary friends as most people would, he tells of Michelangelo who worked concentratedly and for such long periods at a stretch that when at last he pulled off his socks, much of the flesh of his toes came too. He talks of Leonardo's jealousy for Michelangelo, and Beethoven's for Mozart. It is very refreshing. He also has strange bits of knowledge about certain animals in the desert who cannot afford to spare the water from their body, and who urinate in the form of little pebbles. When discussing his family and relations he is interesting about their likes and dislikes which though similar take various forms.

September 8th

We discussed all the most suitable foods we could bring on a hike like this: those that would weigh the least and be most economical in space.

Kin had been reading *Moby Dick* for the third time. He said: 'Ed Kaufman teaches one not just to run along with the story, not to anticipate the author, but to wonder where he is going, why certain key phases are there, and what they signify. Moby Dick is man's attempt to find his soul, by fleeing from the land, going from an island to the sea, and after all these terrible things happen he feels cleansed enough to come back to earth to start life on land again. After the course with Ed, it's like re-reading with new eyes.'

COLE PORTER

September 17th

Cole Porter had set himself on fire. He has taken six months to recover enough to ask people to dinner. Fred Astaire and I were his guests tonight. Cole sat looking like a little celluloid imp, with his one remaining leg propped up on a chair in front of him. He wore a surgeon's white coat and was incredibly pink and clean. He looked rested and wide-eyed like a child, but the delicacy of his frame and the thinness of his hands is terrifying. However, his spirits seemed better than when I last saw him, when he had groaned and gone to sleep at intervals throughout the evening. Tonight he was quiet but alert and interested, and whenever he made a remark it was a pertinent one. Fred was at his nicest, talking about the problems of retirement. He is now sixty-four and too old to dance. He said that physically it was painful, that one was always being brave — 'going on' with a stretched cartilage or twisted fibre; that one was always kicking a piano or having an arm broken by a heavy lady partner. A lot of the talk was about new and old theatre.

Fred has weathered the years well, and I've never known him be less 'cagey'. In the past he was always afraid to commit himself and was rather a bore, though devastatingly attractive. With no axes left to grind, he is calm and pithy, and tonight kept the conversational ball rolling.

Cole's household is run like a hospital-cum-hotel, with a fleet of male servants who tend the patient with care and solicitude.

Our dinner was first class. Stupidly I drank a second rum cocktail and knew this would give me a hangover. It did.

Cole enjoyed his evening immensely, so did I, and it was good to know that I need not have dreaded seeing him.

VISIT TO LAS VEGAS

November 6th

Italians are deliciously serene and vague. At the time we should have left the hotel (quarter-past-four in the afternoon) they were still sitting elegantly finishing lunch and talking of the English portraits and the French furniture in the Huntington Library.

However, we made the aeroplane. We were going to Las Vegas; six of us, my friends the Brandolinis, and other friends of theirs, an enormous amount of luggage and boxes of *bijoux*. The aircraft bumped its way over the desert, and we thought our last minutes had come. However, we arrived, and were met by three men who escorted us to a most luxurious suite in the Sand's Hotel. We all exclaimed at the incredible, vulgar pretentiousness of the decoration: single beds, each the size of the biggest double; imitation trees, and pagodas in the sitting room; fruit and flowers from Frank Sinatra.

Then to our round of pleasures. We were thrilled to get to the slot machines, where in turn most of us hit the jackpot, and to eat a hamburger in a coffee-shop where two Lesbians were the centre of our interest: one with yellow hair and mascara eyelashes, dressed as a young boy in a grey-flannel suit. The fantastic display of lights down-town was beautiful in a vulgar way and a complete revelation to me. The colours were so translucent that the great walls of turquoise bulbs became azure. Broadway's lights were nothing in comparison. Some of the gambling dens were decorated in the style of the 1890s and had little charm, and the strip where the great entertainers perform was not as vulgar as I thought it would be; it is like Miami Beach. However it is an extraordinary place. The Italians were like children and adored every moment of the long evening.

Jerry Lewis is a man with talent, no taste and mighty little charm, but we enjoyed his act. Bobby Darin, an ugly boy with a good way of singing, was our midnight choice. Although he went on, as usual, much too long, we stayed to cheer. Frank Sinatra is the greatest draw today; Belafonte second.

By 2.30 I had to tear myself away as, aching from every limb, I had to get some sleep before a 6.30 am call to get me back at the studio late in the morning. The trip was worth the effort and the expense. I would never go again. As the Brando's said, it is now a *démodé* place to visit.

Hollywood: November 14th

Malcolm Sargent came with me to the film studio. He is not a friend, and in spite of his undoubted wit and vitality, his intelligence and drive, I do not like him. He is appallingly conceited and says things to honour himself that curl one's toes. However, there is no denying his force and he was extremely understanding of all my problems and the obstacles that had to be overcome. He was taken round to see the various studio sights while I got on with the photographic chores of the day.

At dinner at Bina Rothschild's, Malcolm Sargent dominated the conversation. When he taunted a woman by telling her all her stories were exaggerations, or plain lies, some tried to laugh. But I found him intolerable; yet just as I could bear it no longer, he would say something witty and profound. He is a disturbing influence.

Bina is sweet and well-bred. The atmosphere of her house is calm and cultured; but there isn't much stimulus to be found here.

November 22nd

Betsy, my beloved secretary, came back with her nose twitching in its habitual way like a rabbit. 'There's the most terrible news. President Kennedy has been assassinated in Dallas, Texas. He was shot while driving in a motorcade.' My blood turned to a pale liquid; I felt I was rushing through space down a lift shaft. The switch from life to death, the waste, the tragedy for his family, for the country, for the world, appalled me. There was a great sense of shock. I could only grieve for Jackie.

Jack Kennedy's wit, style and courage, his kindness and feeling for humanity, and his sense of humour were his chief qualities. That this young man, at the height of his power, and holding out such promise for his country, should be violently struck down now was an unfathomable tragedy. We were all completely stunned.

NEW YORK

November 27th

I tried Greta again. She had been waiting for my call; then upset to find one of her receivers off the hook. 'That's life,' she said. 'No, it is too late now'; she'd had a glass of vodka — too late to dine.

November 28th

Greta, whom I've not seen for a year, seemed half her usual size, her body completely flat, her face shrunk, her hair shredded with grey. But she looked beautiful and she was as funny as usual. We decided not to walk in the crowded, ugly park but to relax upstairs. She talked of a gloomy summer; how as a result of her films being revived and going well, she was hounded by the Press. By degrees Greta became more cheerful, smiled, and said: 'This needs a celebration. You have no idea how happy I am now.'

I was touched to see her high spirits. She reminisced about London, saw it all through the rosiest spectacles, the house at Pelham Place, the figs at Reddish; Mr Burton; the Election party. It was all so sweet. Greta said we had had a lot of fun, as much fun as possible for people of opposite sexes; perhaps she would come to England again. I was very touched and pleased.

London: November 29th

Real luxury to have Cornelius bring in a tray with blue and white china dishes containing yoghurt and charcoal biscuits served with the newspapers and *Paris Match* and *New Statesman*, etc. A new dimension of luxury to be among one's own possessions.

Friends telephoned. Then lunch with Diana Cooper; a typical group — Caroline Paget, Lindy Dufferin, Moura Budberg, a nice person called Mossman from TV, Rupert Hart Davis; rough and wroughty conversation. Diana winking and joking about her old age; talk about the new President, the ghastliness of the Dallas police; poems of Thomas Moore recited — a treat. The food personal, original and economical; as usual melon and avocado and dill, and a fish pie. Then the big event of going down to Broadchalke.

A NOTE TO THE READER

If you have enjoyed Cecil Beaton's Memoir enough to leave a review on **Amazon** and **Goodreads**, then we would be truly grateful.

Sapere Books is an exciting new publisher of brilliant fiction and popular history.

To find out more about our latest releases and our monthly bargain books visit our website:
saperebooks.com

49404789R00157

Made in the USA
Columbia, SC
20 January 2019